Daring Different

Daring Different

The SCL Seoul Clinical Laboratories **Story**

First edition October 7, 2024

ISBN 979-11-92907-56-7　　03320

Published by yemmibooks in 2024

#B102, 256, Gangseong-ro. Ilsanseo-gu, Goyang-si. Gyeonggi-do,
Republic of Korea
82-31-917-7279 / 82-10-4387-2538
yemmibooks@naver.com
www.yemmibooks.com

Printed in Korea

Daring Different

The SCL_{Seoul Clinical Laboratories} Story

Lee Kyoung Ryul

YEMMI books

Words of Recommendations

For a long time, Korean medical care has competed on a par with global counterparts. However, the potential for creating national wealth through the pharmaceutical and medical device industries, which embody the value of advanced medical care, has been underrealized. The impressive performance of Seoul Clinical Laboratories both domestically and internationally during the coronavirus pandemic marked a significant achievement that mitigated previous disappointments in Korea's medical industry. The 40-year history of Seoul Clinical Laboratories, marked by overcoming challenges and a passionate ambition to advance into the global market in the often-overlooked field of laboratory medicine, will guide us toward a future path for Korea's medical and related industries.

- **Wang Kyu-chang**, Director of the National Academy of Medicine of Korea

This book chronicles the journey of SCL, how it started out as Korea's pioneer testing agency and how it has been providing world-class medical services ever since. Its significance is akin to reading the history of laboratory medicine in Korea. I hope SCL continues to advance as a top-tier institution in medical and medical science.

-**Yu Kyung-sun**, Chairman of Eugene Group

The history of SCL, as detailed in *Daring Different* , vividly illustrates how SCL was able to realize 'one-stop medical care' from diagnosis to prevention. I hope this story reaches everyone in related areas of the industry.

-**Yoon Doh-joon**, Chairman of Dong Wha Pharm

Chairman Lee Kyoung Ryul's management philosophy at Seoul Clinical Laboratories, which boasts world-class technology in laboratory medicine, embodies a spirit of challenge and a commitment to social contribution. This book is an insightful read not only for professionals in medical and business fields but also for the general public, showing how to turn challenges into opportunities and achieve global excellence.

-**Yoon Dong-sup**, Chairman of the Korean Hospital Association; Senior Vice President for Medical Affairs and Medical Center Director, Yonsei University

This book encapsulates 40 years of Seoul Clinical Laboratories and offers a reflective look at the evolution of laboratory medicine and preventive medicine in Korea. It will provide readers with a glimpse into the future of Korean healthcare through SCL's journey of challenges, setbacks, and successes.

-**Rim Che-min** Advisor to Lee& Ko Law Firm, Ltd.;

the 49th Minister of Health and Welfare

Since its inception in 1983, Seoul Clinical Laboratories has significantly contributed to the development of the laboratory medicine field in Korea. Alongside the Korean Association of Medical Technologist(KAMT), SCL has transformed numerous crises, including the COVID-19 pandemic, into opportunities for greater advancement, promoting Korea's exemplary laboratory medicine technology globally.

Daring Different published on its 40th anniversary, allows readers to trace SCL's impressive legacy.

-**Jang In-ho**, President of the Korean Association of Medical Technologist(KAMT)

For the past 40 years, Seoul Clinical Laboratories (SCL) has not only spearheaded the development of laboratory medicine in Korea but also forged global partnerships to shape the future of laboratory medicine institutions in the country. Through substantial investments in universities and healthcare organizations, and talent development projects, SCL has solidified its status as a pioneering social enterprise. I think this book is essential reading to understand the core philosophies and contributions that Korean companies can offer to society and the nation.

-**Jeon Byeong-yul**, President of Korea Public Health Association

Reflecting on SCL's 40-year history through this book, I've witnessed the evolution of Korea's laboratory medicine. I highly recommend this book to those who aspire to lead in advanced medical science and global healthcare.

-**Jun Hye-sook**, National Assembly Member

Leading the Way for a Healthy and Happy Future for Humanity

What kind of organization is SCL?

If asked to describe SCL, many factual descriptions come to my mind: Korea's first specimen testing institution, home to the largest laboratory in Asia, the first in Korea to introduce the PCR test, the first to receive CAP (College of American Pathologists) certification, and the first Korean institution to receive an order for COVID-19 testing from overseas medical institutions. However, if I were to encapsulate it all in one sentence, it would be: "A medical institution that helps people live healthy and happy lives."

While some may find it somewhat unfamiliar due to the nature of our organization, all members of SCL are unified in this vision. For 40 years, SCL has consistently pursued this single path.

SCL is dedicated to performing tests essential for the diagnosis and treatment of patients. We adhere to evidence-based medicine (EBM), integrating objective scientific evidence with clinical experience in patient care. Though the concept may be unfamiliar to the general public, it deeply influences the lives of everyone globally. When we visit hospitals or clinics, whether we're ill or for routine check-ups, doctors rely on tests conducted by specialized agencies like ours to assess our health and diagnose any conditions. Treatment plans are then based on these test results.

Since its inception in 1983, SCL has been committed to fostering healthy and happy lives. As a specialist in laboratory medicine, I firmly believed in the potential of evidence-based medicine from the start. However, this was not a widely- accepted approach at the time, and choosing to follow a path that was barely recognized—let alone well-trodden—was not easy. But driven by sheer passion, I persisted. The stories within this book represent the culmination of 40 years of dedication, not just by one individual, but by all members of SCL who have shared both the triumphs and challenges. These narratives reflect the collective journey of a team unified in striving toward a common goal.

As we commemorate SCL's 40th anniversary, I am filled with anticipation for what the next four decades will bring. Our goal now extends beyond Korea's borders; we aim to showcase the excellence of our country's laboratory medicine to the world.

American actress Audrey Hepburn once said, "Success is like reaching an important birthday and finding you're exactly the same." Echoing her sentiment, I believe SCL will continue to succeed because our founding mission—to help people live happy and healthy lives—remains as clear and compelling as ever. This unwavering commitment has never left my sight.

"The knife you hold must be one that saves people." This profound reminder from my medical school days still resonates with me. SCL began as a specimen testing agency, and now, it has evolved into a comprehensive healthcare group. Although the roles of doctors and entrepreneurs are different, the sanctity and weight of life are constants that I deeply appreciate.

Everyone deserves the right to live happily while safeguarding their health. At SCL, we are dedicated to making this a reality for every individual on this planet.

May, 2023

Lee Kyoung Ryul, Chairman of SCL Group

Contents

Chapter 1   A Road Not Taken by Others

Chapter **2** **Like Iron Refined by Quenching and Tempering**

Chapter 3   The Key to Excellence

Chapter **4** **Diamonds Pulled Out of the Mud**

Chapter **5**   **The World of Dancing Stars**

A ROAD NOT TAKEN BY OTHERS

The path not taken by others is less safe.
But the less safe path grows a company.
A company that takes chances creates history.

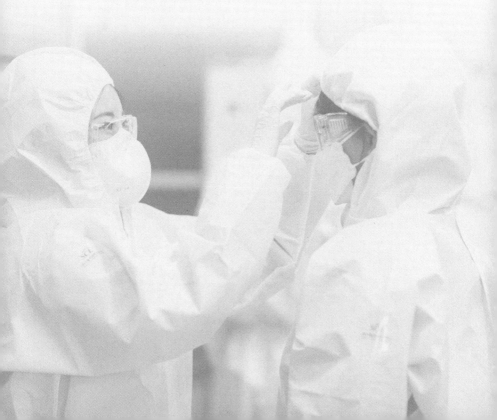

FUNDAMENTAL QUESTIONS ABOUT HUMANITY

SHOUTS ECHOED THROUGH THE ANATOMY LAB

"Stop that and just leave. Now!"

Professor A's yell reverberated throughout the lab. It shattered the concentration, like thinly frozen ice being broken by an ice pick. The medical students gathered around the practice table turned their heads and looked in the direction the professor's finger was pointing. B was there, his hand holding the scalpel, shaking. The professor yelled again at B, who was faltering.

"You just killed the patient. Do you think you're still qualified to hold a scalpel? Get out now!"

B put down his scalpel and took a few steps away from the table before he walked out of the lab. As B disappeared out the door, Professor A's face became expressionless again.

Professor A, who taught anatomy, was known among his medical students for his thoroughness. He was as sharp as the blade of a surgical scalpel (A scalpel for practice is blunt, but the scalpel for actual surgery is quite sharp). His perfectionism shone particularly bright during hands-on training when students personally dealt with cadavers. He never tolerated so much as a single mistake or the slightest negligence.

Anatomy practice, which medical students consider the most impressive experience, is conducted in a more rigorous atmosphere than any other class. In the 1980s, medical school anatomy practice involved one cadaver assigned to every 10 medical students. (There was a shortage of cadavers back then, but even now, more students are practicing on one cadaver.) Medical students engage in practical training with deep appreciation for the noble sacrifice of those who willingly donated their bodies for the advancement of medicine.

On the first day of the practicum, medical students arrive at school in their neatest attire. Before starting the full-scale practicum, they observe a moment of silence in front of the cadaver (Some medical schools even hold separate memorial services to honor the wishes of the deceased who donated their bodies). The cadavers, with whom medical students work, were once breathing, alive, and dignified individuals. Anyone, whether they've aspired to be doctors from an early age or entered medical school on their parents' recommendation, is sure to feel humbled when standing before a cadaver.

When students first encounter a cadaver, they are often scared and troubled, and some may even faint. However, as time passes and they become more familiar with the process, they become engrossed in understanding the mysterious structures and functions of the human body. Under the professor's guidance, students are assigned roles: some hold the scalpel and perform dissections, others consult anatomy books to verify the structures and names of each part, and some lead the overall process. Anatomy practice greatly assists in directly observing the body structures they have learned about in books and in understanding the functions of each part. Since it is unquestionable that anatomy is important as the foundation of modern medicine, medical students are compelled to invest significant effort in understanding every nook and cranny of the body during their practical training period.

The problem is that mistakes inevitably occur during this process. Precisely separating tissue is not as straightforward as it might seem; a moment's lapse in concentration can lead to accidental cuts to nerves, muscles, or blood vessels. Anatomy professors often do not tolerate these mistakes lightly. Professor A, for instance, required students to raise their hands and self-report whenever they made a mistake, and he dismissed those who reported their mistakes. He reprimanded student B for incorrectly handling a blood vessel.

"If you handle a blood vessel like that, the patient could die. Remember, a small mistake by a doctor can cost a patient their life!"

None of those present in the class said it aloud, but they all thought to themselves: Now B will have a grueling time writing and submitting a report. Professor A 'punishes' students who make mistakes during practicum by requiring them to write a report on the body part where the mistake occurred. Students might think it's unfair, but strict education is inevitable due to the nature of the doctor's job. Report writing is an effective punishment because it helps students grow by studying the names and functions of the body parts they mishandled.

Even students who did not make mistakes during the practicum cannot feel at ease, as there is an anatomy practice test. In this test, each part of the cadaver on the practice table is numbered, and students are required to write down the relevant terms and functions within a time limit. Students pore over anatomy books and medical dictionaries, memorizing thousands of terms before taking the exam. They pull all-nighters to prepare for the test, but it is soul-consuming to write down answers while racing against time. Medical students undergo this rigorous training to learn about the human body before they become formal doctors. Perhaps all courses in medical school aim to teach the severity of life.

Watching his classmate being kicked out of the class, medical student Lee Kyoung Ryul recalls, "I felt like my hair stand on end even though I wasn't the one who made a mistake." He understood why his teacher, Professor A, was being so thorough. While learning dissection, he became acutely aware that he was truly dealing with human life. He realized that hidden in Professor A's strict teachings was a deep message: "If we do not handle cadavers carefully, how will we treat living bodies in the future, and how can we protect life?"

"That was probably the first time I really wanted to know how not to make mistakes as a doctor."

People cannot be perfect. Humans are beings that fundamentally make mistakes. But doctors must strive for perfection, because they deal with people's lives. A doctor's mistake is a 'risk' where the ultimate victims are the patients. This presents a contradiction: human beings cannot be perfect, so how can we bridge this gap?

He deeply engraved his teacher's words on his heart: "The knife you hold must be a knife that saves lives." He thought that one day, when he became a doctor, it would be great if he could find ways for doctors to reduce mistakes, make accurate diagnoses, and treat patients. This vague resolve later solidified and began to be realized through Seoul Clinical Laboratories.

PRACTICING THE HEALING ART OF MEDICINE IN A DOCTORLESS VILLAGE

Medical students struggle with an enormous amount of studying. Two years of pre-med is merely a warm-up before stepping onto the main stage. Upon entering medical school, students adhere to a schedule even tighter than that of a high school senior studying for a rigorous college entrance exam. Every day, they arrive at school at 7 a.m. to start the day and attend classes until 8 or 9 p.m. Each month, there are regular exams for each subject, and weekly, there is a "ding test" or "tag test." This test involves questions about dissected parts with tags; students must answer before the bell goes "ding" within just a few seconds. The test, provided by the professor for each subject, is guerrilla-style, with no prior notice of the date and time, and the level of difficulty is quite challenging.

Professors surprise students with random, unannounced tests, and the results significantly impact the students' grades. Students who neglected their studies even slightly during normal times, or those who stayed out late the night before, were severely affected. Thus, medical students must always remain vigilant and constantly study, facing each year as a series of relentless tests. The evaluation method is strict, and advancing to the next grade is not easy. Over 50% of students fail to advance from the first to the second year of medical school, and less than 50% graduate within six years. Most students attend school for about seven years before graduating.

His only hobby was tennis. He enjoyed playing whenever he had time at the tennis court on the campus of Yonsei University's Sinchon College of Medicine. At the time, some of the medical school professors also enjoyed tennis as a hobby, and he was fortunate enough to play tennis with his professors. The professors he met outside the classroom were quite different from those inside the classroom; they were open-hearted and shared stories that would be helpful in their careers.

He said that he received a lot of advice from professors during practicum and on the tennis court, but he found it challenging to decide on a major due to his interest in many fields, such as psychiatry and plastic surgery. Eventually, he graduated from medical school in six years in 1985, passed the national examination, obtained his medical license, and then joined the military.

As a public health doctor, he was assigned to Hoengseong-gun, Gangwon Province. He hoped that he would find his specialty while caring for patients as a public health doctor.

Hoengseong-gun in 1985 was very different from what it is today. Back then, it was a town without a single officially licensed doctor, and the medical gap was filled by the so-called "Hanji Doctor," who was licensed to practice only in a limited area. Once he was assigned and arrived in the town, the hanji doctor wrapped up his work and moved to another town, and Dr. Lee began practicing medicine at a public clinic alongside a midwife who also served as a nurse.

"Once they found out that a real licensed doctor was in town, they came to the clinic in droves. Every day I had to work with no time for a break."

At the time, the population of Hoengseong was about 20,000. When the market was held, every five days, about 250 residents came to visit him daily. There was a serious shortage of hands since there was only one nurse. Elderly visitors had to wait for hours to get their medicines. He explained the situation to the mayor of Hoengseong and introduced an automatic medicine packaging machine for the first time in the history of Hoengseong. This initiative helped reduce the waiting times for patients.

He accomplished more during the second year of public service. At that time, the government was actively carrying out the maternal and child health center project, and he consulted with the town mayor to apply for and receive approval to establish a maternal and child health center in Hoengseong. He went to the obstetrics and gynecology department at Wonju Severance Christian Hospital and received childbirth training for two months. Thanks to this, even though he was not an OB/GYN doctor, he was able to deliver babies without a single accident or mistake at the newly established maternal and child health center.

While he was there, the public health center and maternal and child health center were crowded with people coming even from nearby areas. Because there was a shortage of hands, more staff were added, and a public health branch was opened. In his third year as a public health doctor, he pioneered the health branch in Dunnae-myeon, Hoengseong-gun. At the health branch, he worked with a dental specialist. The mayor of Hoengseong often bought meat to treat the medical staff who worked hard every day. He spent those days working hard and eating happily.

"I can't forget the three years I worked in Hoengseong," he recalls. His time as a public health doctor left such an impression on him, because he felt rewarded for the first time as a doctor treating many patients. Patients who received his treatment grabbed his hand and said thank you, and some showed their appreciation by bringing him sweet potatoes or steamed potatoes from their home. He said, "I was really happy to see the faces of patients who were relieved that their pain was getting better," and "It was also a moment where I experienced the importance of examining and treating patients without making mistakes as a doctor." The experience in Hoengseong served as an opportunity to reinforce the resolve that he had vaguely formed during his days as a medical student.

He returned to medical school after completing his assignments as a public health doctor, and after careful consideration, chose laboratory medicine as his major. Life as a laboratory medicine specialist was opening up another world to him.

THE CORNERSTONE OF DECISION-MAKING THAT SAVES LIVES

What exactly is laboratory medicine? Even today, many people are unfamiliar with it, but people were even more unfamiliar with it in the 1980s. People understand that doctors treat patients and manage diseases in areas such as internal medicine, pediatrics, obstetrics and gynecology, and surgery, but they were less familiar with other medical specialties. The same was true for students aspiring to become doctors. Even now, there are not as many laboratory medicine specialists compared to other medical specialties.

Laboratory medicine is a branch of medicine that originated within the Department of Pathology but became an independent field in 1980. It involves analyzing molecular and cellular components in patient samples such as blood, urine, stool, and body fluids. These analyses are used to diagnose diseases, identify treatment options, and estimate patient prognoses. These analyses are used to diagnose diseases, find treatment methods, and estimate prognoses. Laboratory medicine specialists are comprehensively responsible for everything from selecting tests, collecting and handling samples, to analyzing and interpreting results, and managing and utilizing these results to help clinicians find the most effective treatments. Laboratory medicine is the discipline that "reduces doctors' mistakes and aids in making accurate diagnoses and treatments," a concept he has been dedicated to since his medical student days.

Although it is a discipline not a widely known to the general public, it is extremely important as it underpins doctors' decision-making to save lives. There are many different types of tests performed in the Department of Laboratory Medicine. In addition to analyzing blood, urine, feces, and body fluids, experiments are also conducted on microorganisms such as viruses, bacteria, and fungi. Laboratory medicine specialists also analyze new viruses, such as COVID-19, which emerged in 2020. They conduct all medical research and tests to help people live healthy lives, including studies on diseases like cancer, genetic disorders, and aging.

What would happen if there were no diagnostic or pathological tests? If the medical staff at the approximately 35,000 medical institutions currently operating in Korea relied only on test, palpation, auscultation, percussion, and clinical experience to diagnose patients, could they ensure patients make a full recovery? It is unlikely. Subjective information can be incorrect, and it is difficult to make a proper diagnosis and find a treatment based solely on such information. Treatment outcomes would vary significantly depending on the individual capabilities of the medical staff.

In the 1990s, a tragedy occurred when a woman in her 50s died during a wrinkle removal surgery at a plastic surgery clinic. The clinic had conducted pre-operative tests on the patient but only checked the results of liver function tests before proceeding with surgery without considering the results of bleeding and coagulation tests. The patient died because the bleeding could not be controlled during surgery. This tragedy could have been prevented if the results of the bleeding and coagulation tests had been examined to determine whether the patient was at risk of bleeding problems due to congenital or acquired causes. Bleeding and coagulation testing is a relatively simple test, but overlooking its importance can lead to irreversible consequences.

'Medical errors' occur during the process of diagnosing and treating patients, and this issue is not unique to one country. A study showed that in the United States, more than 250,000 people die every year due to medical errors. Professor Martin Makary's team at Johns Hopkins University in the United States calculated the average death rate due to medical errors using research results published since 1999 and then applied it to the annual number of hospitalized patients. They found that 251,454 people die every year due to medical errors. (This study only included deaths in hospitals, and the number is expected to rise if deaths in other medical facilities such as outpatient surgery centers and nursing homes are included.)

The medical errors he refers to are 'unintended actions' or 'failures to achieve the intended result.' To be more specific, these include misdiagnosis, omission of required tests, medication prescription mistakes, and system defects.

What Professor Martin Makary emphasized when publishing this research paper in the British Medical Journal (BMJ) is the need to create regulations and procedures that ensure safe systems and prevent human errors to operate medical care more safely. We must remember the saying, "Humans are creatures who always make mistakes, and we should not expect them not to make mistakes." *(Reference: "More than 250,000 Americans die every year due to medical errors," Yonhap News, May 4, 2016.)*

Laboratory medicine is a discipline that helps doctors treat patients without making mistakes and achieve the goals of both patients and medical staff. Evidence-based medicine (EBM) is the medical discipline that recognizes its importance and actively utilizes it.

The term EBM was first coined by Professor Gordon Guyatt, a clinical epidemiologist at McMaster University in Canada. He conducted scientific evidence-based tests while taking into account quantitative data such as the sensitivity and specificity of diagnostic methods. Compared with the conventional indiscriminate testing process, he argued that objective and efficient treatment should be provided by using the former. Professor Gordon Guyatt created a research group called the 'Evidence-Based Medicine Group' in 1992, through which EBM became established in the medical world and spread globally. *(Reference: "Overview of Evidence-Based Medicine (1)," Young Doctor, November 19, 2001.)*

From the late 1980s to the 1990s, while steadily completing his internship and residency courses in laboratory medicine, Chairman of SCL Healthcare Group Lee Kyoung Ryul observed with interest the changes happening in the global medical community. EBM was a concept that he believed must be implemented for accurate diagnosis and treatment.

Before the importance of scientific diagnosis based on diagnostic and pathological tests was recognized, doctors made diagnoses and decided on treatments based on clinical experience. When they encountered cases beyond their range of experience, they sought advice from other doctors they knew. This method goes against the main premise of finding customized treatment for each patient. Since each patient has unique physical characteristics and disease patterns, diagnosis and treatment should be based on the analysis of patient information rather than doctors' subjective experience.

Laboratory medicine is a discipline that helps doctors treat patients without errors and achieve the goals of both patients and medical staff. Evidence-based medicine recognizes this importance and actively utilizes it.

What solidified his interest in Evidence-Based Medicine (EBM) was the introduction of national health insurance in 1989. The national health insurance system, which began with the enactment of the Medical Insurance Act in 1963, gradually expanded its target population with the implementation of the workplace medical insurance system in 1977, but underwent a revolution in July 1989 when self-employed people in urban areas also became eligible. This marked the beginning of an era where all citizens could truly benefit from medical insurance.

The introduction of the medical insurance system brought significant changes to the lives of people who had suffered discrimination in medical benefits based on economic disparities. At the same time, it created new opportunities for doctors. In the past, many doctors worked in hospitals after receiving their medical license, but since then, the number of doctors opening small hospitals and clinics began to increase. Small and medium-sized hospitals and clinics had limitations in having a robust testing system for diagnosis. Consequently, there was an increasing need for professional outsourced specimen testing agencies that provide accurate tests, while allowing doctors to focus on diagnosing and treating patients.

Lee Kyoung Ryul dreamed of creating a world where both patients and medical staff are happy by implementing EBM. He became a laboratory medicine specialist, was appointed as a professor, and started a venture company that developed new drug development support services and disease diagnosis techniques while teaching students. His father, who founded Beomyangsa Co., Ltd., and his uncle, who majored in pathology in the United States, assisted him in managing SCL, a scientific laboratory in Seoul. Established in 1983, SCL is a clinical pathology contract testing agency specializing in receiving requests for sample testing from hospitals, clinics, pharmaceutical companies, etc. A sample refers to blood, urine, stool, body fluids, etc., collected from a patient in a hospital or clinic for the purpose of diagnosing or treating the patient. Once these samples are collected, they are sent to a specialized sample testing agency and tested. SCL was making its mark in the EBM field, which was still relatively new in Korea. He had the ambition to create a professional medical service organization.

"I will create a research center with analysis methods and verification power that will become world standards within 20 years!"

Juggling his teaching duties and running a business, he was so busy that he barely had time to sleep. Despite this, he enjoyed his work immensely and kept moving forward, never feeling exhausted. The EBM he encountered as a professor was different from the EBM he dealt with as a businessman. In his school lab, he often thought, "It would be great to have a testing method like this," and at his company, he was able to make that happen. The desire to extend beyond the academic sphere gradually grew in his mind. Although EBM was not yet widely recognized, he was confident that as fields such as new drug development evolved, the demand for professional laboratory medicine services in analytical and clinical areas would increase. He recognized the boundless possibilities of laboratory medicine before others.

DISCOVER OPPORTUNITIES BEYOND A SMALL GAP

It is essential for a company to have a clear vision for growth and development. Simply put, a vision is an 'image of the future.' It represents what one aims to become or achieve in the future and embodies the company's philosophy. Therefore, companies with a vision maintain a clear direction and exude vitality. Employees can set goals aligned with the vision, focus on their work, and support and collaborate with one another. This not only enhances the employees' capabilities day by day but also attracts outstanding talent from outside. The significance of a vision is even evident in the success stories of global companies. Amazon, the world's largest online shopping mall today, began as an internet bookstore selling paper books. Founder Jeff Bezos had an early interest in the e-commerce field. His vision was to create a system capable of selling everything in the world, online. In 1994, Bezos established a business based on the idea of an online bookstore, a business model that avoids holding inventory. As the online bookstore grew, he gradually expanded the business line to include music distribution and movies, until Amazon became the largest online shopping mall in both name and reality. As of January 2023, the company's market capitalization was $923.555 billion, ranking it 5th in global corporate market capitalization.

Amazon's success is attributed to Jeff Bezos having a clear vision and meticulously crafting a strategy accordingly. Amazon operates entirely on a customer-centric approach. The company's goal is to captivate customers with shorter delivery times, a broader selection of products, and higher discount rates than any other online shopping mall. Who could resist a company that focuses on targeting what customers want most? Amazon's sales volume is overwhelmingly higher than that of later entrants in the same industry. It ranks first in net sales among online shopping malls in the U.S. and is not even comparable to Walmart, which ranks second. As of 2019, net sales were $73.75 billion for Amazon and $19.61 billion for Walmart.

Nowadays, people tend to take Amazon's success for granted, but a quick look at the situation at the time reveals how significant this achievement was. In the early 1990s, demand for personal computers was increasing and the internet was becoming more widely accessible, yet it was a time when the offline market had absolute dominance.

There was no smartphone of the type that exists today (introduced by Steve Jobs of Apple Inc. in 2007). In this context, it was adventurous to choose a business with an eye on the future. Jeff Bezos once said, "I took the less safe path to follow my passion, and I'm proud of that choice." His words help us understand the spirit that is essential for businesspeople.

A CEO should be the first to discover and embrace the company's vision. Since his youth, Lee Kyoung Ryul has constantly observed trends in the domestic and international medical community, identified new opportunities that others were unaware of, and made them his vision. Because he had a clear vision, he was able to present it to his employees concisely. If a CEO is not confident, he cannot effectively lead and grow his employees.

Thanks to the CEO and employees working together under the same vision, SCL has the honor of being Korea's first specimen testing agency and has firmly established itself in the medical market as Korea's leading EBM authority. Medical institutions across Korea are requesting specimen testing from SCL and are paying close attention to SCL's every move.

If asked, 'What is your company's vision?' what would you answer? If you can't think of a response within 5 seconds, you should reconsider how the company conveys its vision. If the CEO and other executives express their vision in vague and abstract terms, and even if they use all the right words, but the substance of what they want to do and how to implement it is missing, you can leave that company without reservation. If you are a CEO who habitually makes that kind of abstract statement, you need to innovate yourself. Otherwise, it is only a matter of time before you are left behind in the fiercely competitive market.

AN EXAMINATION ROOM THAT STAYS BRIGHT 24 HOURS A DAY

THE DAYS WHEN HE KEPT RUNNING FORWARD SOLELY ON HIS OWN TWO FEET

Compared to other countries, Korea has a well-established national health checkup system. Koreans can receive a national health checkup once every two years starting at age 20 (Initial infant checkups occur for babies from 14 to 35 days old, with a total of 7 infant checkups provided for toddlers from 4 months to 7 years old, and student checkups from 6 to 18 years old). You may wonder what process your sample collected during the national health checkup goes through before the test results are handed to you. Let's trace the process through which SCL receives a request for sample testing.

When a sample is collected from a patient at a hospital, a test request form (slip) is filled out with the name of the medical institution, patient information, sample name, test name, etc. Any other necessary information is also included on the slip. SCL sales staff visit hospitals and clinics to collect test requests and samples, which are then entered into the company's computer system. The samples are placed in a dedicated sample box, transported to the headquarters (or to local testing centers in Daegu and Jeju). Every day, when samples arrive from the many requesting institutions across the country, the laboratory opens the package, checks the samples, and conducts tests for each test item. Test results can be viewed online, printed out through a computerized network, or delivered directly by the salesperson in charge. The doctor is notified of the results and informs the patient of the relevant information.

SCL currently operates 12 testing teams conducting more than 4,000 types of tests. These teams include automation operation, diagnostic hematology, molecular diagnostics, clinical microbiology, diagnostic immunology, special analysis, cytogenetics, cytopathology, tissue pathology, human genome, my genome, and special microbiology analysis.

Today, sample testing is carried out systematically and quickly, but this was not always the case. In the early days of SCL's establishment and operation during the 1980s and 1990s, processes were not systematic due to the absence of today's established online computer systems. Back then, only the test name was written on the request form, and salespeople had to manually find and record each reception barcode, a process that was time-consuming.

Testers printed out results using a dot matrix printer and then cross-checked the accuracy of the content. Consequently, test team leaders often had to work until 10 p.m. At that time, the internet was not widely available, so most test results were delivered on paper. SCL's headquarters office was busy daily with calls from hospital directors nationwide. For urgent tests, results were delivered by fax; otherwise, they were placed in a storage box at each regional sales office, from where sales department employees delivered them directly to hospitals and clinics.

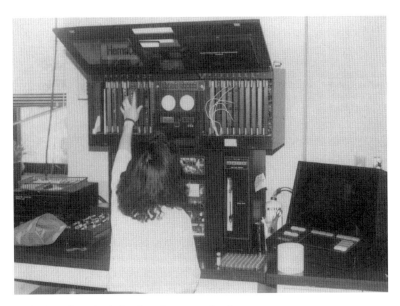

At the time of opening in Insadong, Jongno-gu, Seoul

The methods of transporting samples were also different from today. Now, with the Cold Chain System in place, samples can be packaged and stored at low temperatures to maintain optimal conditions during transportation.

However, back then, such technology or systems did not exist. Salespeople collected samples from nearby clients by walking or using bicycles or motorcycles. When samples came from a local area, an express bus was used. If a sample box was forgotten on the bus, the local sales office personnel would coordinate with the bus driver to retrieve the sample. In cases where the received sample did not arrive, the person in charge at the headquarters would check the shipping invoice with the local on-duty officer and approach the express bus driver to retrieve the sample.

The most frustrating moments for salespeople racing against time occurred when a heavy snow warning was issued. When there was so much snow that vehicles could not move, they abandoned their vehicles and used the subway to transport the samples. In areas without subway access, they waited impatiently for snow removal work to be completed, then delivered the samples by car as soon as the roads were cleared.

In any industry, conditions are likely to be challenging in the beginning. Today, the field of sample testing can be described as a fusion of cutting-edge medical technology and IT, but in the early days, the competition often depended on sheer physical effort. The stories of those who worked hard to reach business partners across the country in the early days of their business are still recounted like legends within SCL.

THE MOMENT TO SPRINT

Anyone who has ever ran knows this: To achieve the best record, you need to not only start well but also manage your speed effectively after the start. If your initial speed is on a par with others, you need to increase your sprint as you progress. You can finish in the first place only if you start sprinting from a certain point and widen the gap between yourself and the others.

Gaining a competitive edge in business is not much different from running. If you start out similar to your competitors in terms of technology or service, you need to accelerate and get ahead. SCL had the honor of being Korea's first independent sample testing agency, but that alone did not provide the company with an edge over the competition. As mentioned earlier, at a time when domestic specimen testing agencies were struggling with inadequate systems, SCL was able to widen the gap with competing agencies by introducing advanced services, such as the night test system and automation system in 1992.

At that time, Korea's specimen testing agencies received specimens separately during the day and at night. Specimens were only received at night (allowing reception staff to leave by midnight), and tests on these samples were conducted the following morning. This was standard practice for testing agencies, but it was inconvenient for hospitals and clinics, as they received test results submitted late at night, much later. When SCL relocated from Guui-dong, Gwangjin-gu, Seoul to Dapsimni-dong, Dongdaemun-gu, the company decided to conduct tests even at night. With the subsequent expansion and relocation to Dongbinggo-dong, Yongsan-gu, the company introduced an automated system for the first time in Korea on the first floor of the building.

The 24-hour non-stop test system and the automated system were both groundbreaking at the time. There were far more sample test requests from hospitals and clinics for nighttime testing than for daytime, and the fact that it took about a day to process them was a major concern for contract testing agencies at that time. SCL established a system that could conduct tests 24 hours a day by recruiting night test personnel and introduced an automated system to accelerate testing times. Subsequently, SCL succeeded in shortening the test time from one day to eight hours. Tests requested before noon could have their

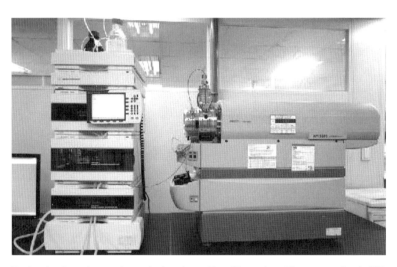

During the time of expansion and relocation to Dongbinggo-dong, Yongsan-gu, Seoul. SCL was able to widen the gap with competing agencies by providing a one-step-ahead service, at a time when domestic specimen testing agencies were struggling with poor systems.

results reported to hospitals and clinics by 5:30 p.m. the same day, and tests requested after noon could have their results reported by 8:30 a.m. the next day. As a result, medical institutions, especially clinics, could now receive results as quickly as if they were operating their own laboratory.

"Our business partners are in an uproar because SCL suddenly started offering nighttime test services."

SCL salespeople encountered complaining protests every time they met salespeople from competing companies while visiting clients in the field. The fact that competitors suffered from client complaints means that SCL's initiative was groundbreaking for hospitals and clinics. Although SCL endured deficits for 10 years from its inception, it was able to grow rapidly through bold and aggressive investments, staying ahead of other contract testing agencies. Currently, among domestic contract testing agencies, there is not a single one that has not introduced a nighttime testing system.

What people want most when they decide to use a product or service is to have their orders executed quickly. It is every consumer's wish to have their orders processed in the least amount of time and accurately and to receive results promptly.

The same applies to hospitals and clinics that request sample testing from specialized institutions. They hope to receive notification of the results from the testing agency as soon as possible in order to provide answers to their patients waiting for test results and to develop their treatment plans. When everyone recognized this need but couldn't find an easy solution, SCL took a risk and embraced a bold challenge, leading to transformative changes in the entire industry.

DOES SCL STAND OUT FROM COMPETITORS?

The term 'Quantum Jump' originates from physics and traditionally means a 'great leap forward.' German physicist Max Planck described a 'quantum jump' as the phenomenon where a quantum, such as an atom, absorbs energy and shifts to a different state not gradually but abruptly at a certain level. In this context, the state in which a quantum absorbs energy is called an excited state, and the state in which it releases energy is known as a ground state. Unlike other objects, quantum changes lack continuity and occur suddenly, as if jumping up or down a stair. For example, if the given energy is 100, there is no change, but with an additional 100, it suddenly jumps to over 200.

Economists have adopted this concept to describe a company achieving rapid, substantial growth or development in a short period, often through significant changes to its business structure or methods. This type of innovative leap is termed a quantum jump. In sports, achieving a seemingly impossible goal is also called a quantum jump *(Reference: Hankyung Dictionary of Economic Terms & Korea Development Institute)*.

Many companies aim to make a quantum jump. Even successful companies are aware that they cannot become complacent, as there might be someone, somewhere, developing technology that could surpass their own. It's surprisingly common for established companies to be overtaken by new startups that can quickly change the market dynamics. That's why it's crucial for companies to develop growth strategies that can substantially outperform their competitors.

To achieve a quantum jump, it's essential to differentiate yourself from your competitors. A differentiation strategy involves gaining a competitive edge by offering consumers noticeable improvements in the nature and technology of products or services. It's about surpassing competitors with unrivaled weapons. Consumers are often willing to pay more for products or services they perceive as distinctively valuable.

Numerous companies have successfully implemented differentiation strategies to achieve a quantum leap. Starbucks is a prime example. Among its several differentiation strategies, one standout approach has been the targeting female customers as its primary demographic. While people of all genders enjoy coffee, Starbucks has tailored its store design, coffee varieties, and service methods specifically towards young female consumers. At Starbucks, customers have the freedom to personalize their orders, choosing from various coffee sizes, shots, syrups, flavors, and types of milk. This customization is often shared on social media, further engaging the consumer base. Limited-edition products like tumblers, mugs, and diaries also see a tremendous response from female customers, often selling out immediately upon release. The popularity of these items is so high that they frequently command higher prices in online marketplaces after they are sold out in stores.

Starbucks does not use a buzzer system. Instead, customers can register their nickname in the Starbucks app. When they place an order in the store, their nickname appears on the receipt. As drinks are served, servers call out customers by their nicknames. This 'Call My Name' service is designed to foster a closer connection with customers. Thanks to the humorous nicknames, both customers and employees often share a laugh.

Starbucks has clearly identified its target audience and developed a differentiation strategy tailored to their preferences. Recognizing that the younger generation enjoys expressing their individuality and engaging with culture, the company has crafted services that cater to these desires in various ways at their stores. This approach is a targeted differentiation, precisely aimed at the lifestyle of today's consumers who are willing to spend as long as they perceive value in their purchases.

This targeted approach has allowed Starbucks to solidify its position as the leading coffee brand. In 2021, a survey by Hankyung Business of 1,000 men and women millennials and Generation Zers (commonly referred as Generation MZ in Korea) about their preferred coffee franchise brand revealed that Starbucks ranked first with 53.2% preference *(Reference: Top 15 brands selected by the MZ generation/ Magazine Hankyung /Oct. 27, 2021)*.

Swedish multinational furniture brand IKEA made waves in the Korean furniture industry when it entered the market in 2014. Until then, major Korean furniture companies had been known for their luxurious materials and designs. Typically, when a customer purchased furniture, it was delivered and assembled by a technician, a service that was included in the price as a sign of premium treatment.

However, IKEA adopted a starkly different approach. Its differentiation strategy was characterized by simple designs, reasonable quality, and affordable prices. Unlike other companies that provided furniture assembly services, IKEA reduced costs by offering do-it-yourself products that customers had to assemble themselves. At IKEA stores, customers select their furniture based on fully assembled models on display, then transport and assemble the furniture at home themselves. Although some customers may think the furniture might not last 10 or 20 years, they appreciate the low prices and the satisfaction of assembling it themselves, reminiscent of putting together a toy in childhood. Other strategic wins for IKEA included adapting the store layouts to fit Korea's residential environment and transforming the shopping experience into that of a complex mall rather than just a furniture store.

IKEA's strategies effectively challenged the prevailing notion that customers prefer extensive pampering. The company successfully established itself in the Korean market by thoroughly understanding customer needs through detailed market analysis. Since its entry in 2014, IKEA has seen annual growth until 2021 (although sales decreased by 10% in 2022 due to the COVID-19 pandemic).

For American IT company Apple, design has been a crucial factor for success. Steve Jobs founded Apple in 1976, but he was ousted in 1985 due to poor performance. When Jobs returned in 1997 during Apple's direst crisis, he prioritized design innovation, famously stating, "I leave the design to the designer and the engineer creates it according to the design." Jobs regarded products as works of art and advocated for a design-centric approach, ensuring technology complemented design rather than the other way around.

Steve Jobs collaborated with British designer Jonathan Ive to create the iMac, which featured a groundbreaking translucent design that captivated consumers with its never-before-seen turquoise exterior.

This was followed by the launch of the iPod, a portable music player that became another major hit for Apple due to its minimalist white design, user-friendly interface, and substantial storage capacity. These innovations helped Apple overcome its managerial challenges and marked a successful turnaround. The success of these products confirmed Jobs' strategy of differentiating Apple through design.

The iMac, iPod, iPhone, and MacBook Air, all developed under Jobs, delivered a fresh shock to the IT industry, which had traditionally prioritized performance and functionality. These products underscored the fact that customers highly value design alongside functionality.

Companies that excel in differentiation strategies can make a quantum leap to industry leadership. For example, SCL stayed ahead in the 1990s by preemptively offering services that hospitals and clinics urgently needed, leveraging a deep understanding of market and customer needs to secure its competitive edge.

Making a quantum jump ahead of competitors brings many advantages. A proactive differentiation strategy can be more cost-effective and less time-consuming than strategies aimed at catching up. By widening the gap with competitors, a company increases customer trust by anticipating and meeting their needs ahead of others, and avoids price wars by sidestepping fierce competition.

Now, you understand the importance of a differentiation strategy for any company. But it's also vital to recognize that not all differentiation strategies guarantee success. Incorrect differentiation can jeopardize a company's survival. Therefore, it is crucial to employ a differentiation strategy that ensures success.

This raises an important question: What forms of differentiation could potentially endanger a company?

First, over-investment is a common pitfall. Differentiation doesn't immediately result in increased sales; it often takes time for a new product to gain traction with customers. If the investment is too large, a company may not withstand the interim before a new product or service gains popularity, potentially leading to financial collapse.

Second, a company is at risk when the funds invested in a differentiation strategy cannot be recouped. If a product or service is enhanced through differentiation, the price charged to customers should increase correspondingly. It's only fair to seek compensation from customers for the enhanced service. However, if the revenue expected from customers falls short of the investment costs, the company remains at risk. To avoid this, both investment and recovery costs must be accurately forecasted at the outset of establishing a differentiation strategy. Moreover, the strategy must be compelling enough that customers are willing to pay a premium.

Third, it poses a risk to a company if it believes it has differentiated its product or service, but this is not perceived by the customers.

If a company fails to accurately understand customer needs and implements a differentiation strategy that is seen as meaningless, it will not succeed in commanding a higher price. In such cases, all invested resources are likely wasted.

Differentiating in these ways will not foster company growth. A differentiation strategy that leads to a quantum jump must be grounded in a deep understanding of what customers truly desire. Furthermore, it is crucial to assess whether the innovation is essential for the business's operation. If a strategy meets these conditions, it merits the full investment of the company's capabilities and taking the calculated risk.

Differentiation means venturing down an unexplored path ahead of others. Taking the first step into unknown territory is challenging, requiring significant capital investment and manpower. Existing employees may have to take on new responsibilities. The journey is fraught with difficulties and the outcome is uncertain, which is why many companies hesitate, even though they recognize the need for a differentiation strategy.

Nevertheless, companies must embrace this challenge. Avoiding innovation out of fear only results in falling behind the competition. Although SCL experienced unstable management during its early years, it gained a significant competitive advantage by steadfastly pursuing a differentiation strategy. Had SCL allowed its initial managerial challenges to deter its commitment to differentiation, it would not have achieved its current status as a leading global medical institution.

Instead of becoming complacent and imitating competitors, it's essential to forge your own strong competitive edge. You significantly increase your chances of success by creating something entirely new rather than merely following in the footsteps of others. Remember the well-worn but vivid truth: 'Opportunities come to those who are prepared.'

THE VALUE OF BEING THE 'FIRST'

HOW DOES ONE COME UP WITH PIONEERING IDEAS?

"I was the first to do this."

Startups and success narratives often highlight individuals who dared to be the first, earning public admiration and personal pride for initiating something entirely new. Being the 'first' in the world (or Korea) or 'top' is impactful because it distinctly showcases one's identity and value. A comedian once lamented, "It's a damn world that only remembers first place." Despite the jest, it's a poignant reflection of society's deep admiration for pioneers. Such individuals are often described with glowing terms: 'overcame numerous adversities,' 'spared no effort,' 'sincere,' 'excellent.'

In corporate settings, being known as the 'first' or 'top' in a field significantly boosts consumer trust. Nothing attracts customers more than knowing who leads the market in delivering exceptional service or products. This drive propels companies to aim for the title of 'No. 1 in the industry,' much like athletes who strive for a gold medal, knowing their achievements will make them shine most brilliantly. Even if rankings change over time, the moment they make history is forever etched in people's memory.

SCL has claimed the illustrious title of 'first' multiple times. The company was the first to introduce night-time testing services and implement an automated system. There are a few other cases that highlight the company's excellence as a leading specimen testing agency.

The first is the introduction of Korea's inaugural PCR (Polymerase Chain Reaction) test. Developed by American biochemist Kary Banks Mullis in 1983, PCR is crucial for diagnosing genetic and infectious diseases through DNA analysis of bacteria, viruses, and fungi, thanks to its ability to significantly amplify specific genetic materials. Mullis received the 1993 Nobel Prize in Chemistry for developing this technology.

After its development, Mullis transferred the patent rights to the U.S. company Cetus, which applied for a patent in 1985. The technology was subsequently acquired by Swiss company Roche for $300 million, who then commercialized it, making PCR available worldwide. This technology has been instrumental in identifying infected individuals during health crises like the MERS epidemic and the COVID-19 pandemic.

From today's perspective, it seems natural for specimen testing institutions to adopt PCR testing. However, this was not always the case. While laboratory medicine was becoming a contentious issue overseas, it remained relatively unfamiliar in Korea, and its importance was underrecognized, even by university hospitals. In 1992, SCL introduced PCR testing and established a molecular diagnostics research center, heralding a new era in Korea's laboratory medicine field, driven by the recognized potential for growth in molecular diagnostics.

The second is the certification SCL received from the College of American Pathologists (CAP), a first for Korea. Founded in 1946 in the United States, CAP is the largest institution of its kind globally and consists of American diagnostic pathologists and scientists. It aims to set standards for clinical pathology laboratories to ensure the highest quality of diagnostic results for patient treatment.

In 1961, CAP developed a laboratory standardization and certification program and has been awarding certification to clinical pathology laboratories worldwide since 1962. These laboratories must undergo rigorous evaluations across various domains, including testing performance, facilities and equipment, employee management, and safety standards. Being certified by CAP signifies that an institution meets international quality control standards for clinical pathology laboratories.

SCL was the first in Korea to obtain CAP certification in 1998. Beyond this milestone, SCL has consistently engaged in leading domestic and international certification programs to maintain its competitive edge and uphold high testing standards. These programs include the Korean Laboratory Accreditation Program (KLAP) and ISO 15189. Modeled after the U.S. CAP, KLAP was established by Korean Society for Laboratory Medicine in 1998 to align with Korea's medical environment. ISO 15189 is an international standard set by the International Organization for Standardization (ISO), ensuring that medical tessting agencies meet rigorous technical and reliability standards. It is crucial for testing agencies to achieve these certifications - validating the accuracy of testing, ensuring a safe laboratory environment, and demonstrating the proficiency of testers. By being the first in the country to secure CAP certification, SCL gained significant credibility with hospitals, clinics, and pharmaceutical companies.

How was such foresight possible at that time?
Reflecting on SCL's pioneering efforts, one might ask this question.

It is crucial for testing agencies to achieve these certifications - validating the accuracy of testing, ensuring a safe laboratory environment, and demonstrating the proficiency of testers. By being the first in the country to secure CAP certification, SCL gained significant credibility with hospitals, clinics, and pharmaceutical companies.

The initiative to embrace Evidence-Based Medicine (EBM) in Korea, when its potential was not yet recognized, stemmed from my vigilant observation and study of technological advancements in the global medical community. My approach was not confined to my immediate field; I keenly observed external developments, deeply analyzed them, and considered how these innovations could be adapted to create new value in the Korean market. This perspective reveals that groundbreaking ideas and initiatives are not mere strokes of luck but the result of persistent effort and thoughtful exploration.

Even now, many people are in search of 'something' that will transform their lives and the world. If you are one of those people, the first step is to continually observe and explore the world around you. While people often look for answers in distant places, they are frequently closer than expected. For businesses, the market is where these answers are found. SCL's diligent market observation enabled it to ascend to a leadership position, proudly bearing the title of 'Korea's first.'

THE STRATEGY OF STRIKING FIRST TO DEFEAT THE COMPETITION

Companies that are the first to attempt what others have not often become industry leaders. This position allows them to earn customer trust, enhance brand recognition, and boost sales. They expand their market share at the expense of their competitors, thereby gaining a competitive edge. In economic terms, this is known as the 'first-mover advantage.'

Coca-Cola is a prime example of a company that has enjoyed the longest first-mover advantage in the global beverage market. Created in 1886 by pharmacist John Stith Pemberton, Coca-Cola started as a beverage intended to be both delicious and fatigue-relieving, made from coca leaf extract, cola fruit extract, and various flavorings. Initially, it was sold in drug stores for 5 cents a glass, but it did not receive a positive response. However, following Pemberton's death, Asa Candler, who acquired the rights to Coca-Cola, founded the Coca-Cola Company in 1919 along with Frank Robinson, a former employee of Pemberton. With exceptional marketing strategies that established the Coca-Cola name, brand logo, and iconic bottle shape, they positioned it as a leader in the beverage industry. In 1898, pharmacist Caleb Bradham introduced Pepsi-Cola, setting up a competitive dynamic. Despite this, Coca-Cola has maintained its leading position with a unique taste and branding unmatched by any other beverage company in the world.

Amazon, founded by Jeff Bezos, is recognized for implementing and successfully expanding large-scale e-commerce among the early online shopping mall companies. As previously mentioned, Amazon's sales are so vast that they dwarf those of other online shopping malls in the United States.

Airbnb, created in 2008 by Brian Chesky, Joe Gebbia, and Nathan Blecharczyk, is the first accommodation sharing platform. After the birth of Airbnb, the traditional lodging industry faced a crisis. Although not the first in the world, as similar platforms existed before, Airbnb became a leader in the lodging sharing industry and now boasts the largest scale globally. Despite the emergence of similar platforms worldwide, Airbnb continues to dominate the market.

Netflix is a leading company that popularized the concept of online streaming, allowing users to receive and play movies and TV programs in real time. At the time of its founding, rental stores were popular, and Netflix entered the market with a rental business as well. Believing it would be more convenient for customers to receive DVDs at home rather than visiting a store, Netflix delivered DVDs by mail and eliminated late fees for overdue returns. These innovative services, which differentiated Netflix from its competitors, were well received by customers. However, as the DVD rental business began to decline, Netflix completely transitioned to an online streaming service in 2007.

Currently, Netflix is considered the leader in the OTT industry worldwide. It is estimated that Netflix has about 231 million subscribers globally, with approximately 5 million households in Korea alone *(Reference: Namu Wiki 'Netflix')*. While Netflix experienced significant growth, Blockbuster, once the largest DVD rental chain in the United States, declared bankruptcy in 2010.

Several factors contribute to Netflix's success, including its content, pricing model, and recommendation engine. Initially, Netflix licensed already-produced content, but since 2011, the company has also been producing its own content, tailored to meet consumer preferences. Subscribers who pay a monthly fee enjoy unlimited viewing, and Netflix offers a premium plan that allows up to four people to use the platform simultaneously. The company's algorithm, which recommends videos by analyzing customer preferences through big data, has been well-received as a personalized service.

The strategic importance of outpacing competitors is evident through various company examples. As noted in one of the 12 Annals of Sima Qian in the *Records of the Grand Historian* striking first can be decisive. The text recounts a moment during the second year of the Qin Dynasty's second emperor when farmers, infuriated by royal tyranny, rose up and seized various regions. Upon hearing of the peasant army's victories, Governor Yintong remarked to Xiang Yu's uncle, Xiang Liang, that with everyone in the Jiangxi region rebelling against the Qin dynasty, it seemed that heaven had forsaken Qin. He observed, "If you strike first, you can dominate your opponent (先則制

人), and if you strike late, you will be dominated by your opponent (後則制制)."

Yintong suggested to Xiang Liang that he raise a force with him and Huo Chu as the vanguards and join the peasant army. Xiang Liang, from a noble family of the Chu Dynasty and an expert in the art of war, heard Yintong's proposal. He conspired with his nephew, Xiang Yu, and arranged for Xiang Yu to stab Yintong to death while they were together. Subsequently, Xiang Liang became the governor and advanced to the Jin Dynasty with Xiang Yu as his general.

Yintong knew that the fortunes of the Qin Dynasty were declining and tried to be the first to strike, but Xiang Liang acted faster than him (Xiang Liang was killed in a surprise attack by the Jin army while advancing to the Jin Dynasty). In times of turmoil, fate changes depending on how quickly you can read the currents of the time. Therefore, alliances and betrayals were rampant among ambitious individuals. It was those who "struck first before others" who could defeat the competition and gain power in the end.

Taking the lead can provide a solid advantage. When several companies are competing, the mere words, "That company is the first (original) company," are enough to sway consumers. If the original company continues to maintain its capabilities and meet consumer expectations, customers are unlikely to switch to another company or product. This creates a significant barrier for newcomers who are closely following the original companies. To overcome this entry barrier, it is necessary for newcomers to create a groundbreaking product that captures the hearts of consumers, which inevitably requires significant investment in capital or manpower. The more pressure these newcomers feel, the more solidified the leader's position becomes. All the hard work is rewarded with great customer loyalty and increased sales. The fruit of this labor is sweet.

TO AVOID THE WINNER'S CURSE

It is very difficult to become a leader on the first attempt. However, securing the leader position does not guarantee that the company will continue to perform well indefinitely. Corporate history is filled with examples of companies that vanished despite once being hailed as 'the first.'

Pantech, a communications equipment manufacturer established in 1991, began by manufacturing pagers (beepers) and launched Korea's first text pager in 1994, followed by voice pagers and wide-area pagers. As pagers gained sensational popularity, the company's sales rose sharply. In 1997, Pantech entered the mobile phone manufacturing industry and, the following year, acquired Hyundai Curitel, a company noted for its excellent technology and recognition. While many companies struggled in the wake of the Asian foreign exchange crisis, commonly referred to as "the IMF crisis," Pantech was thriving, taking third place in the domestic mobile phone market.

Pantech's crisis began with the acquisition of SK Teletech (Sky Teletech) in 2005. The debt from this acquisition snowballed, heavily burdening Pantech. Ultimately, Pantech underwent its first workout in 2006 and was delisted the following year. After entering the smartphone business in 2010, it seemed to be reviving, launching new products and conducting aggressive marketing, but it entered its second workout in 2014. In October 2017, Pantech, now a broadcaster and wireless communication equipment manufacturer, faded into history as it underwent the final liquidation process (Currently, Pantech has been revived under the same name, specializing in patent monetization. This new iteration of Pantech has acquired patents that its predecessor owned in the telecommunications field, as well as patents in the wireless communication and AR fields, and is pursuing several patent lawsuits at home and abroad as part of its monetization strategy). Pantech's case illustrates that victory can actually become a curse if a business fails to manage its success properly after becoming a winner.

The concept of the Winner's Curse first appeared in a paper published in 1971 by three engineers, E. C. Capen, R. V. Clapp, and W. M. Campbell. It originated in the 1950s during an auction for offshore oil mining rights in Texas, USA. At this auction, the winning bid was determined to be excessively higher than the actual value, resulting in financial losses for the winning oil companies after the auction concluded. It was named "the winner's curse" because it describes a situation whereby winning the auction results in a loss due to the bid being higher than the asset's actual value, or when the gains are less than expected because the winning bid is below the actual price. *(Reference: Winner's Curse, "KDI Economy Information Center Current Affairs Terminology", Cha Seong-hoon).*

The winner's curse is prevalent in the corporate world. Cases of companies like Pantech, which aggressively pursued mergers and acquisitions only to falter under financial pressure, are quite common. There are also companies that, in their haste to rise to the forefront of the industry, invest in unreasonable options but are unable to cope and face management difficulties.

Why do companies that were once leaders fall victim to the winner's curse? The primary reason is their inability to deviate from established methods of success. After a few initial successes, a CEO might develop a strong belief in their established strategies. This often leads them to overlook the general business rule of always considering customer needs, becoming instead obsessed with their own experiences and self-confidence. When leaders believe their approach is infallibly correct, they become blind to market movements and customer reactions.

The CEO's rigid mindset also affects the team members. It's difficult for employees to sustain passion when management shows little interest in new ideas or innovation. Eventually, everyone falls into a swamp of complacency. The organization becomes unable to adapt and ultimately grows obsolete. It may have once bloomed brilliantly, but it withers because its roots have been severed.

The market behaves like a living organism, constantly changing and evolving. For a company to survive in this dynamic environment, prioritizing an understanding of customer needs is essential. CEOs must abandon the arrogance of believing 'I am the truth' and humbly listen to the voices of field workers, interpreting the deep sentiments of customers conveyed in those voices. The battles a company faces are ongoing; if a leader becomes arrogant, the entire company can quickly fall from the top.

Moreover, even after achieving success, leaders must set new goals and continue to invest in research and development. Without goals, a company cannot grow or retain talented individuals. The CEO must instill a vision in all team members, establish step-by-step objectives, and strive relentlessly.

Efforts to understand customers' needs and to set progressive goals are the best strategies to avoid the winner's curse in an uncertain market environment.

Chapter **2**

LIKE IRON REFINED BY QUENCHING AND TEMPERING

The strength of iron increases through quenching and tempering.
Becoming stronger inevitably involves pain,
but if you overcome it, you can enter a new world.

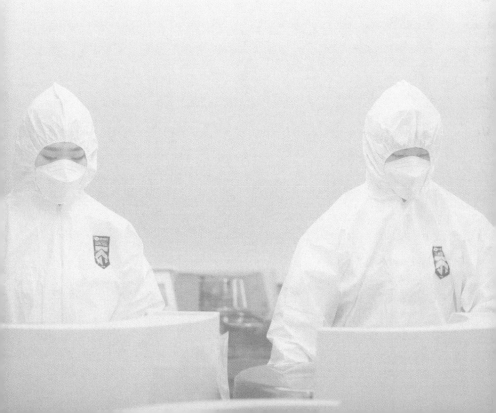

THE CRUCIAL DIFFERENCE BETWEEN FIRST-CLASS AND THIRD-CLASS

ET TU, BRUTE?

I couldn't believe it.

The atmosphere inside the company became uncontrollably turbulent when as many as 20% of the employees left all at once. These employees spanned all departments, including sales, management, and testing—truly, a mass exodus of what could be called 'essential personnel.'

The employees who resigned had not properly completed the handover process. Even if one decides to quit, transferring job duties to successors is a fundamental responsibility, yet even this basic principle was neglected. The remaining employees were left flustered, suddenly shouldering unfamiliar responsibilities left by those who left the company as if chased by someone or swept away by an ocean wave. In their distress, they gathered in small groups, whispering whenever they had a moment. I didn't need to listen to understand what they were discussing.

"At this rate, the company might go under, don't you think?"

This was the prevailing concern among the employees. SCL had previously navigated through management challenges and continued to grow as an industry leader by pioneering several initiatives. These included establishing a nighttime testing service, introducing automation systems, adopting PCR testing methods, and achieving CAP certification.

Yet, just as SCL began to enjoy its heydays, with customer numbers increasing daily and a loyal customer base solidifying, we faced the most severe crisis since the early 2000s. We were brimming with expectations of only walking on a bed of roses, but we hadn't anticipated a crisis capable of destroying our very foundation. The saying "good comes with the bad" rang true, but the impact was devastating.

Why on earth did they quit? Where did they go? The mystery was soon resolved. They all moved to a rival company in the same industry, performing similar work to SCL. There, they replicated a system akin to what SCL had developed, allowing the new company to easily acquire the know-how that SCL had invested considerable time and resources into developing.

How would SCL management and remaining employees feel about it? I don't think the expressions 'flustered' or 'feeling betrayed' are sufficient. It is profoundly painful to see those whom you trusted coldly turn their backs on you, reminiscent of the ancient betrayal of Julius Caesar by Cassius Longinus and others, and his dismayed cry "Et tu, Brute?" upon seeing his adoptive son Brutus among them.

SCL employees were flustered, upset, and angry. Since they were colleagues who had gone through thick and thin together for a considerable time, they felt terrible that they had not considered how the remaining colleagues would feel—flustered and distraught. Anyone experiencing something like this would feel the same way. However, there was no time to remain emotional, because we had to address what was happening right in front of us.

The news that a large number of SCL's key personnel had quit the company spread quickly throughout the industry. Hospitals and clinics that had been steady business partners of SCL were concerned when they heard this news. Due to the improper handover, it was difficult for employees to grasp the details of the tests entrusted to them by business partners, and many complaints arose from partners who did not receive test results on time. Salespeople visited hospital directors one by one to reassure them. Since the work had not been properly handed over and there were no hospital websites or GPS systems like there are now, they had to rely on maps to visit clients, checking each client's address with their business registration certificates and fumbling their way around.

Business partners also asked if SCL was going out of business, because employees who had left the company were spreading negative stories about SCL. Once trust is broken, it is difficult to regain. Sales staff had to work diligently to dispel misunderstandings by explaining the company's situation to concerned business partners and persuading them.

The crisis that SCL experienced in the early 2000s is an event that many long-standing companies may encounter at least once. When your company achieves success in the industry, it naturally comes under scrutiny from those around you. Your employees may receive attractive offers from competitors, and it is only natural for them to consider leaving their current positions. In a highly competitive society, it is unrealistic to expect family-like loyalty from employees.

When you consider it, the above mentioned incident offers valuable insights into how we should think about work. If you aim to be recognized and succeed within an organization, you must consider what your fundamental attitude toward work should be.

A true professional identifies themselves with their work. This doesn't mean living a life wholly devoted to work, but rather valuing your work as much as you value yourself and performing it with a sense of responsibility. It involves taking the initiative, not sparing time or effort to enhance your skills, and ensuring your tasks are completed to the best of your ability. Even when leaving an organization, a true professional ensures that their responsibilities are neatly organized. They keep detailed records and thoroughly brief their successor to ensure a smooth transition. This demonstrates responsibility for one's name, respect for the job held, and respect for oneself, having devoted much of their time there.

People who are sincere about their work earn the support and trust of those around them. Everyone prefers to delegate tasks to someone they can rely on, and conversely, they will hesitate to entrust responsibilities to someone who hastily abandons their current position for new opportunities. Business owners are particularly wary of hiring someone who leaves their company impulsively, as they may harbor concerns that this pattern will repeat. Even if a professional relationship ends, one's reputation continues to influence their career. Remember, if you aspire to achieve great success, it is crucial to present yourself as a professional and manage your reputation meticulously.

LET THE DEAD PAST BURY ITS DEAD!

The news of the crisis that befell SCL reached Lee Kyoung Ryul, who was working as a college professor and running a venture business while also helping to manage SCL at the time. He agonized over how to revive the company and soon made the most important decision of his life: he decided to leave his position as a professor and take over as chairman of the SCL board, following in his uncle's footsteps. He described his new role as a 'fireman' missioned to pull the company out of crisis.

As he assessed the company's situation, he was taken aback by the severity of the issues—it was worse than he had imagined. He set out to find solutions one by one.

The first thing he aimed to address was the pervasive sense of crisis and defeat within the company. He believed the worst outcome would be for employees to lose their motivation to work. It was challenging to immediately replenish the suddenly depleted manpower, so the remaining employees had to manage the workload of three to four people each. In the testing department, for example, the number of tests each employee handled was so high that they endured extreme working conditions, arriving at work at 6 a.m. and not leaving until 11 p.m.

Although it was devastating to lose key personnel, Lee Kyoung Ryul knew he could not afford to dwell on the past. Inspired by American poet Henry Wadsworth Longfellow's words, "Let the dead past bury its dead! Act,– act in the living Present!", he focused on addressing the current situation. While managing his responsibilities, he continuously encouraged his employees and reminded them of his vision whenever he had the opportunity. As management began to pull together and inject new energy into the company, employees also started to overcome their negative emotions. They supported each other, boosting morale and becoming each other's pillars of strength.

All executives and employees rallied for grassroots efforts. To restore the credibility of their test results and reassure business partners that SCL was still operational, they personally visited each business partner across the country. They aimed to collect samples and deliver test results with greater accuracy and speed than before. Sometimes, administrative staff from the headquarters joined the sales team on these visits. They would wait until late at night, approach doctors as they finished their treatments, and plead for a moment of their time. Even though they might only speak for one to two minutes after waiting for hours, the employees felt relieved to have at least met the hospital directors. Through persistent appeals and persuasion, they gradually alleviated the partners' uncertainties, and business resumed as usual. Fortunately, since SCL was the first in Korea to obtain CAP certification, they leveraged this as a marketing tool to assure partners that their quality control of tests was superior to any other institution. The second course of action was to transform the crisis into an opportunity. The keyword he identified as a breakthrough in this crisis was 'innovation.'

Specimen testing is typically done manually. Collecting specimens, analyzing results, printing them, and delivering them to doctors—all these tasks are performed by people. Although the system operates 24 hours a day, its high dependency on human intervention not only increases the time and cost involved but also raises the likelihood of errors in test results. If a large number of employees were to leave the company again, as had previously occurred, it could bring operations to a standstill, let alone compromise the quality of the test results.

"The most important thing is whether we can still meet our customers' needs."

Fast and accurate analysis, a shortened process, and a swift delivery system—these are the core competencies that a sample testing agency must possess. Chairman Lee Kyoung Ryul believed that by harnessing IT technology to achieve these core competencies, he could provide uninterrupted, high-quality services to customers, even if key human resources were lost to competitors. "What is there to be afraid of," he thought, "when we can meet the needs of our customers?"

This conviction led to the creation of an automated system for the entire testing process. This large-scale project, which unfolded over three years, involved every member of the company, from medical specialists to sales staff. Completed in 2002, the system used IT technology to automate the previously manual tasks of sample classification and reception. This innovation not only eliminated the possibility of human error but also significantly shortened analysis time, enhancing both the speed and reliability of test results. Thanks to this fully automated system, the laboratory workload was reduced by as much as 48%, allowing personnel in the testing department to be reallocated to specialized tasks like molecular diagnostic tests, thus improving work efficiency.

In 2005, an advanced online Laboratory Information System (LIS), dubbed 'SMART' (SCL Medical Application Revolutionary Technology), was introduced along with an integrated clinical pathology information system. These systems marked a significant shift from the manual operations prevalent in the sales and testing departments during the 1990s. While basic LIS laboratory medicine systems and purchase billing systems were established in the early 2000s, there had been no major innovations until then. The manual processes—from collecting and testing samples to deriving and delivering results—were complex and time-consuming. By reducing the reliance on human intervention, these systems aimed to enhance customer satisfaction significantly.

Building the SMART system, which integrated systems developed specifically for each department, was not as straightforward as it might seem. At the time, there were not many internal personnel available to develop a company-wide system, and creating a system tailored to the specifics of medical testing was a truly challenging task. In building a clinical pathology information system, cooperation between internal personnel (employees) and external personnel (system development companies) was essential. Even if an IT specialized company took the lead, the role of internal employees, who were familiar with the clinical pathology information system's information, was crucial. Therefore, to facilitate mutual understanding, a clinical pathologist was assigned to the computer system development team. This pathologist helped identify essential test information for the program development and also conveyed relevant system information, such as computer terminology, to the testing department.

SMART significantly improved internal work processes and greatly enhanced customer satisfaction externally. Customers appreciated the ability to quickly and conveniently view and receive test results at their locations.

The automation system built in 2002 underwent a major upgrade in 2008. SCL formed a task force team with Siemens Korea, a global laboratory medicine equipment company, to build Asia's largest automation system, the Laboratory Automation System (LAS). LAS features a 22-meter long track that enables it to conduct a large volume of blood tests simultaneously. Moreover, it analyzes with approximately 1,000 times greater sensitivity than previous testing methods and can test more items (increasing from 39 to 65 items). With the introduction of LAS, the test analysis time was reduced by approximately 2.3 times, enabling real-time analysis of samples and reporting of test results to customers.

Currently, the SCL test department utilizes over 400 types of state-of-the-art equipment for a systematic system capable of conducting over 4,000 testing categories. These include automated operations, diagnostic blood work, molecular diagnosis, clinical microorganisms, diagnostic immunology, special analysis, cytogenetics, cytopathology, histopathology, human genome, personal genome analysis, and special microorganism analysis, among others.

SCL underwent an organizational reorganization alongside the establishment of an automated system. In 2006, the company restructured its organization according to the field and volume of work. A separate team dedicated to research and testing, called C-LAB (Central Laboratory), was formed. Historically, the research testing area was perceived merely as a service provided to customers, often resulting in low fees or even free testing. Naturally, this did not attract much investment. The situation at SCL was no different, and the academic support department in charge of research tests was operated for a truly multipurpose purpose. However, clinical trials related to new drug development were on the rise in the United States, Europe, and Japan. By the 2000s, Korea's Ministry of Food and Drug

Safety and pharmaceutical companies investing in R&D recognized the need for an institution specializing in clinical trials. SCL also received inquiries from companies about specimen analysis for clinical trials. Companies were seeking a testing agencies certified by international standards, and SCL, being the first in Korea to receive CAP certification, was ideally suited to their needs.

Following inquiries from companies, SCL decided to expand the scope of clinical tests and redefine the role of the Academic Support Department. The research testing work was separated from the previously complex tasks such as research test consultation, specimen reception, consignment management, and promotional material production. Two new separate teams were also created: one in charge of national research services and another in charge of clinical testing.

This reorganization plays a crucial role in strengthening SCL's expertise in the field of clinical trials. Subsequently, SCL was able to expand its business scale significantly by securing clinical trial projects from national institutions and pharmaceutical companies. The department responsible for new drug development clinical trial services is now called the Pharmaceutical Clinical Team, part of C-LAB (New Drug Development Support Headquarters), while the department handling national research services is known as the Research Management Team. These departments are precursors to

Currently, the SCL test department utilizes over 400 types of state-of-the-art equipment for a systematic system capable of conducting over 4,000 testing categories. These include automated operations, diagnostic blood work, molecular diagnosis, clinical microorganisms, diagnostic immunology, special analysis, cytogenetics, cytopathology, histopathology, human genome, personal genome analysis, and special microorganism analysis, among others.

what is now the Technology Innovation Center, which includes the national project team and the human body resources teams.

IF YOU CAN SUSTAIN YET DISRUPTIVE

The series of processes through which SCL navigated the crisis in the early 2000s can be categorized as both 'sustaining innovation' and 'disruptive innovation.' This concept was introduced by Clayton M. Christensen, a professor at Harvard Business School. Christensen differentiated between two types of innovation: 'Sustaining Innovation' and 'Disruptive Innovation.' Sustaining innovation involves a strategy to increase market share by incrementally enhancing the performance of existing products and services to align with market expectations, and subsequently offering them at a higher price. In contrast, disruptive innovation is a strategy that seeks to capture the market by initially entering with low-performance but affordable products and services, targeting the lower end of the market, and then gradually improving quality to increase market share. It is termed 'disruptive' because it allows small and medium-sized enterprises, which may lack capital, to shake up the existing market order by targeting segments that mainstream companies have overlooked.

While the original meaning of disruptive innovation pertains to the above description, in the real world, the term has evolved to signify 'innovation that dramatically changes the existing market.' It encompasses enhancing a company's core competencies through changes in the processes of producing existing products and services, technology, organizational structure, management systems, and staff interactions *(Reference: Win-win strategy with disruptive innovative companies, "Technology and Innovation," Nov. & Dec. 2022 issue).*

Many people are curious about which approach − sustaining innovation or disruptive innovation − can make a company more successful. Sustaining innovation is a strategy employed by established companies with a significant market share, while disruptive innovation is typically adopted by smaller or newer companies entering the market. Mainstream companies continue to invest in key areas and charge high prices to maintain their market dominance. However, this can eventually lead consumers to seek alternatives. In such circumstances, if a company enters the market with lower-quality and lower-priced offerings, it has the potential to usurp the mainstream company, especially if it introduces a new paradigm that enhances its disruptive impact. This explains why many people are drawn to disruptive innovation (which may also be partly due to the appeal of the term 'disruptive' compared to 'sustaining').

It is more useful to understand the characteristics of each type of innovation and use them as a reference for corporate strategy rather than debating which is superior. Sustaining innovation allows a company to continue pursuing growth rather than resting on the laurels of existing products and services that dominate the market. Through the ongoing efforts of mainstream companies, customers benefit from enhanced technological capabilities. There are always customers willing to pay a fair price for advanced technology, regardless of the industry, and these customers significantly impact company sales.

However, mainstream companies must be cautious. If they focus solely on sustaining innovation, consumers might shift their loyalty to newer companies, especially if these newcomers introduce new values and address the dissatisfactions of customers who were previously overlooked. Mainstream companies often overlook innovative opportunities due to pride in their long history. While they are quick to gather feedback from influential customers, they tend to disregard the opinions of less impactful ones, missing unmet needs in the market. It's crucial to recognize that such oversights are common in corporate settings.

One company often cited as an example of disruptive innovation is Apple. Apple revolutionized the mobile phone market with the introduction of the iPhone in 2007. This innovation led to a shift in smartphone design, moving from physical keyboards to larger, touchscreen displays similar to the iPhone's. Consequently, some argue that Apple's disruptive innovation significantly impacted the mobile phone market. However, others believe that Apple's true disruption was in the laptop industry. With the introduction of mobile phones that nearly matched the functionality of computers, the laptop market saw a reorganization into categories like tablets and general-purpose laptops. Apple's success illustrates that in the computer market, there are mainstream consumers interested in high performance as well as those who prefer smaller, more portable devices.

The more we delve into disruptive innovation and sustaining innovation, the clearer it becomes that comparing their superiority is meaningless. Companies should not overlook either type of innovation. If a company can effectively leverage both sustainable and disruptive innovations, maintaining a dominant market position and appealing even to the lowest tier of consumers, it is likely to solidify its leading position in the industry.

SCL's journey through its crisis encompasses both disruptive and sustaining innovation. This is evident as SCL enhanced customer satisfaction by establishing systems far more advanced than those of other sample testing agencies, including the automation of the entire testing process and an integrated information system. SCL has effectively upgraded its technology to precisely meet the needs of its major customers.

The decision to create a dedicated team focused on clinical trials, a sector that previously received little attention and contributed minimally to sales, can be regarded as an approach close to disruptive innovation. Major clients were not heavily involved in the clinical trial area. The fact that SCL established a dedicated team and continued to expand it at a time when most other specimen testing agencies were not seriously investing in clinical trials represents a type of innovation that mainstream companies might not readily pursue. It is noteworthy that an institution known for sustaining innovation ventured into disruptive innovation.

Any company can face a crisis. This might involve non-payment from customers, an unexpected fire, or a mass exodus of employees, as SCL experienced. Such crises can lead to the leakage of core technologies to competitors through departing employees. The future of a company is shaped by how it responds to these crises. A failure to effectively manage a crisis can lead to collapse, but successful navigation can propel rapid advancement.

SCL faced a significant crisis but managed to overcome it with distinction. We dramatically innovated existing systems and services, overhauled the organizational structure, identified neglected areas, and developed them into new competitive strengths. As a result, we moved one step closer to our vision of becoming 'the best specimen testing institution in the country.'

Although the initial crisis was clearly unintentional, it was SCL's deliberate choice to transform the crisis into an opportunity. The SCL crisis overcoming story embodies the words of former Intel Chairman Andy Grove, who stated, "Bad companies are destroyed by crisis. Good companies survive them. Great companies are improved by them." A tower built with great effort can collapse. However, with determination, it can be rebuilt even taller.

THE LAST BASTION AGAINST HUMAN ERROR

HUMANS MAKE MISTAKES, BUT HOW DO WE MITIGATE THEM?

From its inception, SCL has been acutely aware of the variable called 'human error.' As a medical institution that provides critical data for treating patients, we cannot afford a single error in the process of generating that data. The accuracy and speed of test results can be life-saving. Consequently, I have been deeply interested in the various mistakes that can occur during testing procedures. How can we fundamentally eliminate this variable?

'Human Error' refers to mistakes made by humans. The reason humans err is due to our physical and mental imperfections. It is fair to say that human history is a chronicle of mistakes. From birth, we encounter countless failures and errors—from learning to hold our heads up, to crawling, standing, walking, babbling, and speaking. Becoming an adult does not exempt one from making mistakes. While the nature of these errors might change, the fact remains that humans are inherently prone to error.

Statistically, humans think about 50,000 thoughts, perform 20,000 actions, and make two mistakes daily. Out of these daily average mistakes, 80% are detected while 20% go unnoticed. Moreover, 25% of these undetected errors and 5% of all mistakes are classified as very serious.

If there are 1,000 workers, it is estimated that 2,000 mistakes occur daily. Out of these, 400 mistakes go undetected, and 100 of these undetected errors lead to serious accidents. *(Reference: Human Error, "Korea Occupational Safety and Health Agency," February 26, 2020).* Direct contributors to these errors include illusions, forgetfulness, memory lapses, unintentional carelessness, and negligence.

Many accidents in industrial settings stem from these human errors. Rather than merely emphasizing the importance of not making mistakes to workers, it is more pragmatic to create systems that compensate for human imperfections. We need to closely examine where and how mistakes can occur and develop methods to fundamentally prevent situations where errors are likely.

From this perspective, it's evident that mistakes contribute to personal growth. Humans, inherently imperfect, can grow significantly when they acknowledge their mistakes and seek alternatives. As the saying goes, one is born imperfect but strives towards perfection.

As a medical institution, SCL was particularly focused on preventing errors during the testing process. The establishment of C-LAB (Central Laboratory), a dedicated clinical trial team, underscored this commitment.

As mentioned earlier, in the early 2000s, SCL established C-LAB as part of its strategic response to crises and its drive for innovation. At that time, there was no central laboratory dedicated to analyzing domestic clinical test samples, making SCL's initiative a forward-thinking decision. This proactive approach was facilitated by the recognition from the Ministry of Health and Welfare and domestic pharmaceutical and life science companies of the need for clinical trials and their desire to find professional and reliable agencies to conduct them.

Since 2004, the Ministry of Health and Welfare has supported the establishment of global leading clinical trial centers within 14 tertiary medical institutions in Seoul, the metropolitan area, and other major cities. Additionally, the ministry operated the National Clinical Trial Support Foundation (KoNECT) to bolster international competitiveness in clinical trials for domestic new drug development. KoNECT works in collaboration with domestic clinical trial centers and clinical trial consignment agencies to lay a solid foundation

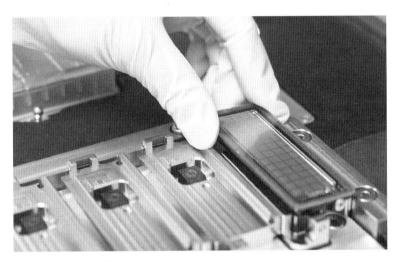

From its inception, SCL has been acutely aware of the variable called 'human error.' As a medical institution that provides critical data for treating patients, we cannot afford a single error in the process of generating that data.

for clinical trials in Korea. It also oversees the entire clinical trial industry, including the development of professional manpower and the attraction of domestic and foreign investments.

These internal and external changes were clearly advantageous for SCL, as it obtained CAP certification for the first time in Korea in 1998 and was also operating a central laboratory. SCL continued to set records, such as being the first among central labs in Korea to obtain Good Clinical Laboratory Practice (GCLP) certification and the first to obtain ISO 15189 in the laboratory medicine area. An increasing number of pharmaceutical companies and clinical trial consignment institutions requested SCL for clinical tests, and they even included requests from overseas companies. Currently, the total number of clinical test projects in which SCL C-LAB participates amounts to approximately 600.

Today, the importance of clinical trials has risen to an unprecedented level compared to the past. The number of clinical tests conducted in Korea increases annually. The Ministry of Food and Drug Safety and KoNECT announced that the number of clinical test plans approved in 2021 was 842, an increase of 5.4% compared to 2020, with steady growth over the past three years (679 in 2018, 714 in 2019, and 799 in 2020). Of the 842 cases in 2021, 679, or 80.6%, were clinical tests led by pharmaceutical companies, marking an increase of 11.1%

compared to 2020 (611 cases) *(Reference: KoNECT clinical test status data)*.

While receiving orders for clinical tests from various domestic and foreign companies, it became clear to SCL that the level of requirements for the scope, process, and overall management of research projects was increasing significantly. Some clients even requested not only research data but also management of records documenting the research process. SCL needed to demonstrate its professionalism and expertise, in addition to acquiring certifications from reputable certification agencies.

SOP COMPLEMENTS HUMAN LIMITATIONS

"When all these changes were happening within and outside the company, I had the opportunity to visit LSIM in Japan on a business trip. It was a revelation for what SCL needed," recalled the head of the clinical test support division, reflecting on his 2006 trip. LSIM, formerly known as MCM (Mitsubishi Chemical Medience), is Japan's largest global CRO (Contract Research Organization) and clinical test consignment agency, established over 40 years ago (as of 2023). He was particularly impressed during his visit, noting that due to the geographical susceptibility to earthquakes, LSIM's building was designed with a low floor height and boasted an outstanding safety management system. This included manuals for responding to natural disasters such as earthquakes and tsunamis, as well as a robust security management system, including entry and exit controls. Though he had always believed SCL was the best in Korea, the visit highlighted that there was much to learn from LSIM's approach to safety and security.

"Due to the country's susceptibility to natural disasters, the company meticulously prepared evacuation and escape routes for emergencies. These routes were clearly marked with yellow arrows."

What struck him most was LSIM's adoption of standardized work manuals. Various job tasks within the company were systematically categorized, and work procedures were organized into Standard Operating Procedures (SOPs). An SOP, also known as 'Standard Operating Guidelines' or 'Standard Operating Procedure' in Korea, is a detailed description of procedures and performance methods aimed at ensuring consistent work execution. It includes basic procedures, execution methods, and outlines for handling different cases. The primary advantage of an SOP is its ability to prevent work-related errors and to effectively manage unforeseen variables. With an SOP in place, consistent results can be expected even with personnel changes. Consider this scenario: Manager A has been in a department for 20 years, and New Employee B has been employed for less than 6 months. The disparity in their experience is vast. However, if an SOP is well understood and adhered to by B, the same outcomes can be expected as if A had performed the task. Ultimately, the purpose of an SOP is to minimize human variability in processes (although it does not replace the judgment that comes from experience, it excels in tasks where process consistency is crucial).

SOPs are crucial in any area where quality control is critical, and he believed they were especially necessary in the field of clinical testing. This stems from the fact that clinical tests involve collaboration among experts from various fields who must work together organically to produce a unified result using the data they individually derive. Due to the inherent complexity and potential complications in this work, a meticulously established standard work guide is key in decisively preventing inspector errors, facilitating cooperation among experts, ensuring quality control, and achieving accurate results.

Furthermore, SOPs are absolutely essential for ensuring the reliability of clinical tests. All processes must be performed according to specified procedures, and it must be possible to verify that these procedures were followed, through records. These records not only detail how tasks were performed but also document the corrections made when mistakes occurred. Improper application of drugs or medical devices can have severe adverse effects on patient health. Therefore, the entire process—from the development of medicines and tests to treatment delivery—must be conducted safely. This is why entities such as the Ministry of Food and Drug Safety, domestic pharmaceutical companies, and life science companies seek certification from tessting agencies and require comprehensive records of the testing process. With SOPs in place, alongside proper certification, customers can maintain unwavering trust in the process. Upon returning to Korea, he resolved to implement SOPs at SCL.

FIGHTING PEOPLE'S PERCEPTIONS

Thoughts often differ from reality. I was convinced that Standard Operating Procedures (SOPs) were absolutely necessary, but not all employees were easily persuaded. They argued, "We already know how to do our jobs. Why do we need a new method?"

The employees, being professionals who have long mastered their roles, naturally found it unnecessary to establish new work procedures. It's like asking an honor student with top grades to switch to a new study method; they wouldn't see the need.

Moreover, the SCL test department already had quality control guidelines, which were essential for conducting tests. Since SCL was undergoing laboratory certification, employees believed they were complying with the appropriate training, facilities, environment, and safety standards for testing—equating this with SOPs. However, while they may seem similar, there's a clear distinction.

For example, during the pandemic, the laboratory's quality control guidelines specified the types of specimens needed for COVID-19 tests and how to handle unsuitable specimens. In contrast, with SOPs in place, procedures were much more detailed: they covered everything from the types of containers used to collect specimens from patients, to collection sites, methods of collection, and handling high-risk specimens. Each step was assigned to specific individuals and managers, along with methods for creating and storing necessary records. It was not about checking each procedure and standardizing them.

SOPs should include detailed procedures for routine tasks and also outline steps to resolve unexpected emergencies. For instance, all responsible parties should collaborate to anticipate potential emergency scenarios, such as improper collection of a COVID-19 specimen. Resolution procedures might include revisiting the patient, canceling the test, replacing the container if unavailable, or actions to take if an employee handling the specimen is exposed to infection risk or confirmed to be infected. Since the purpose of SOPs is to minimize human error, they are particularly effective in emergency situations.

The key challenge was explaining the difference between expanding existing guidelines and adopting the SOPs necessary for the work process. Persuading the employees took a considerable amount of time, and implementing and internalizing the SOPs took even longer. "In a way, it's about changing people's perceptions, and essentially, it involves fighting their existing perceptions to bring about change." Changing people's perceptions is probably one of the most difficult challenges because everyone has their own deeply held convictions. He believed that if everyone understood exactly what SOPs entailed, they would all recognize their necessity.

He aimed to create SOPs for all work processes across various departments in the company, including research, administration, and testing. For instance, the SOPs would standardize procedures for tasks such as planning to open branches overseas, taking steps in international locations, and marketing and promoting the business. Establishing SOPs for each department helps prevent conflicts, duplications in work, and oversights.

It wasn't an easy task as it required gathering information from all departments, and the cooperation of employees was absolutely necessary. He managed to develop the SOPs thanks to his years of experience, which allowed him to understand many aspects of the operations at a glance. Employees who recognized the need for SOPs actively cooperated.

As he noted, the most crucial element in establishing SOPs is the cooperation of the individuals responsible for the relevant tasks.

While someone can lay out the framework, the details must be filled in by those who know the work intimately. The employees contributed to the SOP project in their spare time while performing their regular duties. It was initially awkward to proceduralize tasks that had become routine, and there were times when details were hard to recall, but they supported each other until they successfully established the SOPs.

Later, the Japanese company LSIM commended SCL during a visit. SCL was also able to improve its practices based on their advice.

The initial SOPs that SCL adopted from LSIM in Japan were detailed and included about 250 clinical test processes, many of which were specifically tailored to the local context in Japan. Therefore, the employees undertook continuous revision work to adapt them to better suit SCL's needs. The current SOPs, which are revised and modified annually, are now well-suited to SCL.

The evolution of SOPs continues. The company diligently updates its SOPs to remain in compliance with the standards set by certification evaluation agencies, ensuring the maintenance of both domestic and international certifications. As testing methods evolve and regulations change, it is crucial to revise the SOPs to stay current. He confidently asserts, "Other medical institutions also strive for quality control, but it would be challenging for them to maintain a department as dedicated and professionally managed as SCL's."

A MOMENT WHEN TRUST FROM MANAGEMENT IS ESSENTIAL

"I am nearing retirement, but my dream is to see all departments proficiently working through properly implemented SOPs while I am still in office," he shares with a bright smile. His wrists are wrapped in bandages due to carpal tunnel syndrome, a condition he developed from relentless work without rest, compounded by his poor two-finger typing skills.

He fondly recalls the company's supportive response when he first proposed the need for a central laboratory and the establishment of SOPs after his business trip and visit to LSIM in Japan. He meticulously outlined how establishing a new business division and practicing SOPs could significantly expand SCL's operations. Upon hearing his proposals, management immediately supported him, encouraging, "Do whatever you feel is necessary."

"They all recognized the importance of objective and scientific data. Yet, creating a new department at an employee's request is not a decision management can make lightly," he acknowledges. He expressed his gratitude for being able to work happily, thanks to the company's active acceptance of his suggestions.

In fact, clinical tests constitute a small fraction of SCL's overall business, accounting for less than 10% in terms of both the number of tests conducted and revenue generated. Despite this, the required records and process management are extremely labor-intensive and time-consuming. Naturally, one might question the rationale behind dedicating significant resources to a segment that contributes minimally to the overall business. Without company-wide commitment, resistance from various departments is inevitable.

"Given that clinical tests are a minor part of SCL's business, creating SOPs related to them can seem like a tedious task. However, it is also true that SOPs ensure the reliability across all business areas of SCL." With strong support from management, all departments and employees came together to embrace the concept of SOPs, which was initially unfamiliar to them. Chairman Lee Kyoung Ryul commented, "By establishing SOPs, SCL has enhanced its credibility as a specimen testing agency. This achievement stems from our trust in our employees and our unwavering support." The SCL case has since become a role model for many companies and organizations seeking to establish SOPs in the clinical testing arena.

Jack Welch, a renowned management expert, once said,
"My job is to place the best people in the most promising businesses, select the right businesses to invest capital in, provide ideas, allocate resources, and then step back and not interfere. A great business leader is someone who knows when to stop managing." *(Reference:*

Leadership Secrets From Jack Welch by Robert Slater)

A great leader is not necessarily someone who excels individually, but rather someone who places the right person in the right position. This is a long-standing definition of leadership. A lone wolf leader may thrive independently, but they cannot foster growth within the community. In contrast, a leader who nurtures the talents of employees and paves the way for their development can help the entire community prosper. This occurs because seeing passionate employees inspires others. They progress together as a community, moving toward a shared vision while supporting and encouraging one another.

In many companies, CEOs assign tasks with the mindset of "I am the truth." They claim to be open to employees' opinions, but in reality, this openness is merely lip service, as they fail to act on employees' suggestions. In such environments, it is exceedingly difficult to find employees who are proactive and innovative. They tend to remain passive and uncritical toward management, finding contentment in maintaining their positions and receiving regular paychecks rather than seeking a better direction for the community.

If you aim to be a wise leader who can cultivate both people and organizations, you must first acknowledge your own limitations. Instead of imposing your thoughts and opinions on your employees, pay attention to those who approach work differently. Trust them and give them the opportunity to fully utilize their capabilities. As long as a CEO uses their authority to suppress employees and micromanages every aspect of their work, there will be no room for talent or growth within the organization.

WHEN ABRUPTLY CONFRONTED

WHO RANG THE PHONE?

That day, a call to the customer service department left the employees distressed. It was from a patient at a certain hospital, and he was clearly upset. While receiving calls from hospitals or clinics is common—they are our clients—receiving calls directly from patients is unusual. Upon contacting the hospital that requested the test, we learned that the patient had become quite agitated after hearing his test results from the doctor. He made a fuss, demanding to know where the test was conducted. Subsequently, he contacted SCL directly, and later, his family members also called, unleashing a barrage of angry words.

We wanted to clarify the results until the patient could understand and accept them. However, since the explanation from the testing agency and that from the hospital must align, we set aside our frustration and advised them to consult directly with the hospital. The staff responsible for the test results called the hospital to explain the findings in detail, ensuring the information would be accurately relayed to the patient.

"Just because we explain things well doesn't mean that issues will always be resolved smoothly. This is because patients sometimes receive results they do not want to hear."

Among the complaints, some cases are particularly complex. For instance, we received an inquiry concerning the test results of a young female patient involved in a legal dispute with a hospital. She had undergone a biopsy at a tertiary hospital and was diagnosed with cancer. Previously, she had been assured there was no issue with a test conducted at a local OB/GYN clinic. However, after her cancer diagnosis, she filed a lawsuit claiming the initial test results from the local hospital were incorrect. Distressed, she contacted SCL to protest the alleged inaccuracies in her test results.

What stance should we adopt in such challenging situations? Our employees unanimously agree that we must present the facts based on objective data, setting aside emotions. For instance, the aforementioned patient was tested through a screening test provided by the local hospital, designed to differentiate people with a specific disease from those who are healthy. Since our agency analyzes exfoliated cell smears, it's impossible to determine health status based on anything other than the specimen itself.

Despite our adherence to protocols and the accuracy of our testing, patients often reach out to the agency to appeal or protest, venting their anger and frustration over an undesirable diagnosis. Complaints are common, and in some instances, individuals even confront our staff in person. We've had instances where a patient's guardian, in a moment of distress, attempted to physically assault an employee. Such incidents deeply demoralize our team, making it difficult for them to function throughout the day. "Wouldn't anyone feel overwhelmed if hit with a complaint like a bolt from the blue?" you might think, empathizing with them, yet it's hard not to feel disheartened, as if all your diligent work has been for naught.

If our explanations fail to assuage the concerns and we continue to receive harsh complaints, we sometimes resort to sending the test results to an overseas testing agency for an independent review. It is only when we provide the objective data confirmed by a third-party that the emotions of all parties involved tend to subside.

Our customer service employees are trained to communicate scientifically, not emotionally. Yet, as they face various scenarios, they learn to adapt their responses. Sometimes they engage with patients rationally and scientifically; other times, they offer sincere comfort. The more they interact directly with the diverse reactions of patients, the stronger their sense of mission grows.

When the test department staff are notified of an incoming phone call by the customer service team, they momentarily pause their work. Calls from outside the department often set their hearts pounding, inducing a sense of nervous anxiety. New hires feel this most acutely, wondering, "Is this a complaint?" or "Did I make an error in the testing?"

"For some reason, I can often intuitively sense if the call is about a specimen I tested. I think my perception has sharpened over the years due to my experience." Despite their scientific training, their accuracy in anticipating such calls is almost uncanny.

The test department staff spend their days deeply engaged with specimens, which are not only the subjects of their analysis but also akin to their partners and friends. Compared to other departments, they interact less with outsiders. Nonetheless, there are times when external calls are directed to them. Business partners might reach out through the customer service department or sales office, seeking further details about test results, expressing dissatisfaction, or requesting expedited results. Test results are rarely straightforward. Often, multiple results need to be comprehensively interpreted, or tests conducted by analyzing photos or images may yield ambiguous interpretations. Consequently, there are frequent inquiries from business partners regarding these results.

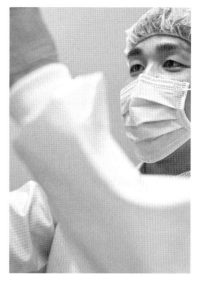

Even with automated systems handling various tasks, human oversight remains crucial. Staff must verify specimen integrity, ensure machines function correctly, and accurately interpret results.

If asked which department at SCL operates under the most pressure, it would undoubtedly be the test department. The nature of their work leaves no room for human error. Even with automated systems handling various tasks, human oversight remains crucial. Staff must verify specimen integrity, ensure machines function correctly, and accurately interpret results. Given the potential for errors—such as similar patient names with different birth dates—rigorous double and triple verification procedures are a standard practice to prevent mistakes.

One of the most challenging aspects of working in the test department is the unpredictability of the workload. Just because you processed 10,000 tests today doesn't mean tomorrow will bring the same number—it could be 20,000 or even 30,000. Since test results must be delivered within the promised timeframe, employees must remain vigilant from the moment they arrive until they leave. By labor intensity alone, few other jobs match the extremity of this one.

Even typically manageable situations can escalate into problems when sensitivity runs high. Disagreements sometimes occur among employees as they discuss test results. It's understandable, as not everyone thinks the same way, and each person brings their own expertise and pride to their work.

"Sometimes we get mad, but we get over it later. It happens because everyone is trying to do their job. Once we move past it, we tend to understand each other better."

There's little more nerve-wracking for those already sensitive about their work than receiving phone calls.

New hires are reminded by their team members to approach each test as if it were for themselves or a family member.

"If we discover a patient is ill through testing, it means we are potentially saving their lives. But if we overlook something, the patient could be put in danger. Therefore, we must stay alert. The tester has to see the patient beyond the specimen."

Once an error becomes known, the credibility of the organization can plummet dramatically. Since a small mistake by one person can threaten a patient's life and jeopardize a business relationship, all employees must embrace a sense of mission and responsibility.

Like iron that strengthens the more it is tempered, the testers continue to focus intensely on their work, regardless of the many unforeseen events that challenge them.

INTEGRITY OVER PROFIT

What qualities define a good tester, according to the testers themselves? The testing laboratory is a place where unexpected events can occur frequently. Therefore, one should not choose this profession solely because they excel at analyzing and interpreting test results. A tester needs a sense of mission and responsibility towards life, coupled with sincerity, concentration, meticulousness, and the ability to cooperate. Naturally, possessing the appropriate qualifications is essential to excel in this role.

Testers, armed with various qualifications and expertise, often possess a strong professional pride. This pride serves as a motivational force that drives them to perform even better in their roles. As the saying goes, these are individuals who are not swayed by money.

An illustrative incident occurred when a researcher approached SCL to conduct a test that would support the hypothesis of their paper. Maintaining credibility is paramount in the experimental process, especially when the results are intended to validate a research hypothesis. The SCL test department carried out the test, but the results contradicted the researcher's hypothesis. Subsequently, the researcher demanded a re-examination, not in search of error correction, but aiming to have the results align with his expectations. He subtly pressured the test department, hinting at potential problems with the payment of test costs if his desired outcomes were not achieved.

The staffer in charge reported this unethical request to their superiors,

One should not choose this profession solely because they excel at analyzing and interpreting test results. A tester needs a sense of mission and responsibility towards life, coupled with sincerity, concentration, meticulousness, and the ability to cooperate.

leading to a decision to terminate the researcher's test and reject any future requests from him. Similar incidents have occurred, but each time, the testers have adhered to scientifically derived results without compromise. Even if such decisions might negatively impact sales, management stood firm without regret.

Yielding to client demands for tailored results might offer temporary benefits, but it would undermine the employees' pride and morale. Moreover, it contradicts SCL's commitment to evidence-based medicine, an ethos that stands at the core of the company's values.

The management and employees of SCL can work with pride and a sense of mission because they collectively value their work's purpose over monetary gain. This is evident from the many experts, each with over ten years of working in the same company, spread across the various teams within the SCL test department. The sense of pride among department members is further boosted by the company's significant achievements: building the largest automated system in Asia, comprising about 400 laboratory medicine devices and 4,000 testing items, and conducting an average of 100,000 tests per day. Moreover, the company continually introduces new testing systems for conditions like latent tuberculosis and rare, incurable diseases, and constantly strives to enhance the testing environment.

THE PRECARIOUS LINE BETWEEN PRIDE AND BURNOUT

A few years ago, an advertisement resonated well with viewers. In the ad, an employee rapidly fires questions at a customer at the checkout counter, asking if he has mileage, a point card, or if the cardholder is his mom or dad. Watching the employee, the customer thinks, "I don't want to do anything. I'm already doing nothing, but I want to do nothing even more intensely."

This sentiment might echo the feelings of SCL's testers who return home exhausted after a day of intense focus and passionate work.

The definition of burnout is "a state of physical and mental exhaustion caused by prolonged stress or frustration." Burnout syndrome refers to extreme physical and mental lethargy experienced by individuals who have devoted all their energy to work, feeling as if they have been completely drained, or "burned out." Symptoms of burnout include persistent fatigue even after rest, poor appetite, sleep disturbances, loss of motivation, irritability, anxiety, and a general sense of being overwhelmed by everyday tasks.

Employees in the SCL test department take immense pride in their work, recognizing its impact on saving lives. However, the intense workload and the meticulous nature of their duties often lead to significant stress. Among their greatest challenges, these employees cite "neglecting their families" as a prevalent issue. No matter how sociable or talkative they may be by nature, they find themselves quieter and withdrawn after enduring the demands of their daily responsibilities. Completely drained by the end of their shift, they often return home only to collapse on the sofa or bed, struggling to engage even in simple play with their children.

"I need to rest now to be ready for tomorrow's challenges. Even though I can't always interact with my children as much as I'd like, just seeing their faces recharges me."

Each employee in the SCL test department has developed personal strategies to cope with stress, which they often share with colleagues. The most common methods include sleeping, taking walks, and chatting with peers. One employee remarked, "Despite the exhaustion, the positive feedback from clients brings a deep sense of pride and fulfillment."

SCL has maintained relationships with hospitals and clinics for over 20 years, enduring through various management crises. These enduring partnerships boost employee morale. Clients also take pride in their mutual development with SCL as well.

The challenges faced by SCL inspectors are not unique to them; they are common among office workers worldwide. While striving for excellence at work is important, it is equally crucial to avoid burnout. According to a survey by the global recruitment consulting firm

Robert Walters, conducted across 31 countries, 82% of respondents reported experiencing burnout even before the COVID-19 pandemic. The shift towards remote work has further blurred the lines between professional and personal life, exacerbating the workload and increasing burnout risks. Many employees report heightened stress due to constant directives from supervisors via messaging apps *(Reference: 6 Ways to Prevent Employee Burnout, Robert Walters Korea).* Burnout not only diminishes individual happiness but also impacts corporate competitiveness. As a result, companies are increasingly focused on preventing employee burnout. SCL is enhancing its efforts in this area through employee training and improved welfare programs (this will be detailed in Chapter 5). Implementing company-wide burnout prevention strategies is crucial for maintaining healthy relationships with employees, protecting their well-being, and building trust within the company.

In 2013, the German automobile company Daimler implemented the 'Mail on Holiday' system, which deletes emails sent to employees on vacation. Senders receive a notification that their email has been deleted, with options to redirect the message to another employee if it is an urgent matter or resend it once the original recipient returns. This system ensures employees can enjoy uninterrupted vacations while keeping business operations flowing.

The travel and airline consulting firm Simply Flying has introduced a mandatory vacation policy, where employees work for seven weeks and then take the eighth week off. During their vacation, work-related contact is prohibited, and any violation, such as working secretly, results in non-payment for that day *(Reference: Introduce mandatory vacations to eliminate burnout syndrome, Security News, February 12, 2020).*

Researchers at the Emotional Intelligence Center at Yale University analyzed the correlation between high engagement and potential burnout among employees. Their findings were published in a paper titled "Highly Engaged But Burned-out." They analyzed 1,000 American workers and found that approximately 20% of respondents were 'engaged-exhausted.' This term describes those who perform well due to high engagement but are also at a high risk of burnout. From an organizational perspective, there is a concern that these excellent performers might leave due to burnout *(Reference: Reduce the workload of high performers and distribute work evenly, Economy Chosun, August 11, 2018).*

To retain talent, companies must strive to change their work culture rather than view burnout as merely a personal issue. As demonstrated by the initiatives at the aforementioned companies, working outside of regular hours should generally be prohibited. It is crucial for companies to monitor workload distribution to ensure it is fair and reasonable, provide a proper salary system, and offer compensation that reflects performance. Most importantly, fostering an internal communication culture where employees can openly share work-related challenges and have their opinions considered is essential for maintaining a healthy work environment.

When management actively engages in these efforts, employees are more likely to trust their employer and remain with the company over the long term.

While challenges can be formative, it's important to recognize that human energy is finite. Corporate management should avoid overburdening employees with the expectation that they grow through hardship alone. Inspiring employees with a clear vision is crucial for achieving results, as is creating a system where talented individuals can thrive without becoming exhausted. Ultimately, such strategies are not only beneficial for the employees but also enhance corporate competitiveness.

Chapter **3**

THE KEY TO EXCELLENCE

Excellence is not about settling for today but looking toward tomorrow.
If you overcome the sweetness of the present,
you will meet a future incomparable to the past.

TOWARDS A NEW WORLD

THE EASIEST WAY TO OPEN PEOPLE'S HEARTS

It was 10:00 a.m., and there was only one hour left until the opening ceremony.

The head of the global marketing department hurriedly left the venue and headed to a nearby mart. His destination was a batik shop in the mart (Batik is an Indonesian technique of wax-resist dyeing applied to whole cloth, and the traditional Indonesian clothing made from this patterned fabric is also called batik).

In July 2022, SCL Healthcare had been preparing to enter the Indonesian healthcare business sector with LX International for several months. That day marked the finale of a long journey, and a large-scale event was scheduled. The event aimed to introduce Korean laboratory medicine by inviting local medical staff from Indonesia and was one of the largest such events hosted by Korean companies in Indonesia. SCL specialists and experts were set to present Korea's laboratory medicine capabilities, the K-LAB model, and the latest laboratory medicine trends that would interest local doctors.

He could proudly say that he had prepared meticulously, but he still wondered, 'Is there anything else we can do?' The event was designed to showcase Korea's laboratory medicine technology in a foreign country. It was unfamiliar territory for the hosting company, and he assumed the local attendees might feel the same. Wanting to bridge the cultural gap and approach them in a friendly manner, he noticed the attire of the local and Korean employees of K-LAB preparing for the event–they were dressed in batik, the traditional Indonesian costume.

'Yes, that's it!' he thought.

As soon as the rehearsal concluded, he dashed to the market, purchased a batik, and quickly changed into it. Though he had specially prepared a business suit for the event, he felt no regrets about switching his attire. Donning the batik, he finally felt fully prepared and ascended the stage with renewed energy.

The event was a resounding success. The Indonesian locals were visibly moved, commenting, "We were touched." They appreciated that even the Korean employees had donned traditional Indonesian costumes, recognizing the depth of sincerity in the preparations.

The department head's extensive experience in international business had taught him the importance of cultural respect when entering new markets.

"I've been to many Middle Eastern countries, including Iran and Saudi Arabia. In Iran, I wear a scarf on my head, and in Saudi Arabia, an abaya. In this way, our employees adapt to resemble local women. Regardless of the debates surrounding the hijab, such gestures express our goodwill toward the country as someone who is there for business."

His aim in Indonesia was to convey this same goodwill. Understanding that business is fundamentally about people, he believed that genuine connections could pave the way for success. The event's atmosphere was imbued with warmth and appreciation, filled with praise for Korea and its cultural exports like K-pop.

This episode underscores a vital lesson for Korean companies looking to expand abroad: to succeed internationally, it's crucial to win the hearts of the local people and earn their trust.

Then, how do you persuade others effectively?

The *Difficulties of Persuasion* section in Han Feizi, written by the philosopher Han Feizi during the Warring States period of China, offers foundational insights. Han Feizi defined persuasion as "understanding the other person's mind," highlighting that true persuasion is inherently challenging. According to him, the difficulty lies not in a lack of knowledge, eloquence, or boldness, but in the complexity of truly grasping another's mindset and tailoring your persuasive efforts accordingly. Han Feizi advocated for a persuasive approach that respects the other person's thoughts and avoids provoking their emotions.

This philosophy underscores the attitude of employees who diligently work to expand business internationally. Rather than relying on elaborate rhetoric or eloquent speeches, they prioritize showing genuine respect for others. Such simple actions proved sufficient to win the hearts of Indonesians, demonstrating that opening people's hearts does not require complex strategies. Respect and consideration can bridge vast cultural and geographical divides, making even strangers in distant lands feel understood and valued. This anecdote illustrates that the essence of effective persuasion, especially in a global context, hinges on empathy, respect, and a deep understanding of the other party's perspective.

IF YOU WANT TO GO FAR, GO TOGETHER

When someone remarked that the person in charge of headquarters seemed to enjoy his work while he passionately explained SCL

Healthcare's foray into the Indonesian market, he shook his head and responded that, even though the project was progressing smoothly, it was not always enjoyable.

"There's a lot to prepare meticulously since we are collaborating with many partners."

SCL Healthcare's entry into Indonesia began through a partnership with LX International, a leading Korean conglomerate with extensive operations in Indonesia. Learning of the Indonesians' high interest in healthcare businesses, including Korean laboratory medicine technology and laboratory services, LX International approached SCL for a consultation before entering the lab business in Indonesia. After reviewing market trends and government policies, SCL Healthcare decided to enter the healthcare sector.

The head of the global marketing department, through his travels in the Middle East, including Iran and Turkey, had confirmed a global need for healthcare services. Encouraged by the growing demand and the expanding specimen testing market in Indonesia, Chairman Lee Kyoung Ryul decided to make a serious push into the Indonesian market.

In early 2022, after three months of preparation with LX International, Chairman Lee established SLX in June, marking the start of their mission to introduce Korean laboratory medicine technology to Indonesia and establish K-LAB.

The initiative was actively driven by the project team. In October 2022, the head of the headquarters test department traveled to Indonesia as the Chief Operating Officer (COO), tasked with overseeing the company's internal operations. The Korean and Indonesian staff conducted weekly video conferences to monitor progress.

"LX International has extensive local experience, from which I have learned a great deal. Our visions for the healthcare business align well, creating synergies that enhance our collaborative efforts."

The sentiment expressed by the head of headquarters resonates with the African proverb, "If you want to go fast, go alone. If you want to go far, go together." Collaborating with another entity requires more time and effort than working independently. Had the two companies pursued their international expansion separately, they might have saved on the costs of consulting and cooperation. However, they would have lacked the combined strength needed to achieve the ambitious goal of developing overseas markets. By uniting under a common vision, SCL Healthcare and LX International were able to approach the market development with greater vigor than they could have individually.

In December 2022, SLX's K-LAB received its official license from the Indonesian government (Izin Lab Utama, Ministry of Health). The Indonesian K-LAB facility spans an independent four-story building—housing a reception, emergency room, and pharmacy on the first floor; a screening center on the second; office space on the third; and the laboratory itself on the fourth. The staff included medical, administrative, and logistics personnel. While the Indonesian K-LAB was largely modeled after SCL's facilities in Korea, the specimen transport logistics system had to be modified due to differences in healthcare processes between the regions. In Korea, testing agencies operate branches nationwide, collecting specimens directly and transporting them to labs for analysis. Conversely, in countries like Indonesia, and other parts of the Middle East and Southeast Asia, the process is more decentralized. Here, residents take prescriptions from hospitals to collection centers, which then send the specimens to labs. After analysis, the results are sent back to the collection centers where residents retrieve them.

Recognizing the unique challenges posed by Indonesia's complex road networks and frequent traffic congestion, SLX's team innovated a logistics system tailored to these conditions. Instead of relying on cars, they opted for a more agile solution—motorcycles. The team equipped the fleet with two cars and about 10 motorcycles, conducting thorough simulations to optimize specimen collection routes and pickup times. Their proactive outreach included visits to 670 hospitals to promote the lab and secure testing contracts.

In January 2023, the Indonesian K-LAB officially commenced operations. The sight of motorcycles zipping through the streets, efficiently transporting specimens, sparked curiosity among the local populace and instilled a sense of pride in the SLX team. While the future was uncertain, the present was filled with confidence. The vision of K-LAB becoming a cornerstone of healthcare in Indonesia, embodying the Korean-style testing agency's responsibility, seemed within reach.

A LEAP TOWARD A WIDER WORLD

For successful companies in Korea, the progression from domestic leadership to international expansion has become almost a standard. But why this push to enter overseas markets? The primary motive is the pursuit of new growth opportunities.

Today, SCL's capabilities far surpass those from a decade ago. Few countries boast a testing system as well-developed as Korea's, and among Korean testing agencies, SCL stands out as a leader. The scale of SCL's testing labs, the quality of equipment, the expertise of personnel, technology, and cold chain systems are comparable with those in the most advanced nations.

A key factor in the development of our country's specimen testing technology has been the robust health insurance system. Koreans enjoy access to hospital treatment and care without undue concern about costs, and the government also offers them a health checkup every two years. This system, envied by many, inspired the United States to adopt a similar approach with 'Obamacare,' modeled after Korea's framework.

SCL began as the Seoul Medical Research Institute, a specimen testing agency, and has since expanded into a diverse medical platform. This includes the Hanaro Medical Foundation for screening, Q-Logic for IT solution development and diagnostic reagents, AhealthZ specializing in MRO, Bio Food Lab for food and livestock product quality inspections, and SCL Therapeutics for new drug development. The growth of these sectors was greatly facilitated by Korea's advanced health insurance system, which is unparalleled internationally.

For companies with expanded capabilities like SCL Healthcare, Korea's domestic market is relatively small. Considering the country's overall market size and population, it's challenging to achieve significant growth by only competing domestically. Expanding into larger international markets and scaling up business operations are essential for higher sales and increased influence.

SCL Healthcare has strategically sought to establish a presence in overseas markets. The company's first international venture was in Mongolia, where it established Mongolmo Bio, a specialized testing institute in Ulaanbaatar in 2003, introducing advanced medical technologies and the latest diagnostic techniques. The second step was China, where in 2013, SCL launched the first Korean-style comprehensive screening center, Han Nou Medical Checkup Center. Indonesia marked the third significant international market entry. By leading its overseas expansion with highly competitive business divisions, SCL has managed to maintain its market competitiveness without resorting to price reductions.

FOUR CONDITIONS FOR SUCCESSFUL OVERSEAS EXPANSION

Overseas expansion is a natural and essential process for companies seeking growth. However, not all ventures into foreign markets succeed. Successful outcomes typically depend on several key conditions. SCL Healthcare's success in international markets can be attributed to four primary factors.

The first factor is the thorough analysis of the target overseas market. This includes detailed research on the market size, as well as the characteristics of the people, politics, economy, society, and culture of the country.

For example, due to the lack of birth control policies in Muslim countries, there is a high birth rate, necessitating a focus on prenatal examinations and tests for pediatric diseases. Another example is Mongolia, where there is a high rate of hepatitis C virus (HCV) infection, largely due to the prevalence of nomadic lifestyles. HCV is mainly transmitted through blood, and at the time SCL entered Mongolia, there was no routine testing of blood donors (SCL had to evaluate the suitability of donated blood in a similar way to practices in Korea). Consequently, recipients of blood transfusions were at high risk of contracting HCV. To address this, MobioLab prioritized setting up HCV PCR testing, significantly reducing the HCV infection rate. Such precise tailoring of business strategies to fit the specific characteristics of each country dramatically lowers the likelihood of failure.

Some Korean medical institutions have attempted to enter foreign markets without such meticulous preparation and have not succeeded. Given the significant differences between domestic and overseas markets, success is challenging without a comprehensive analysis and the rapid establishment of a targeted strategy.

The second key to success in overseas expansion is securing a domestic partner who is deeply familiar with the local context. Regardless of how extensively a company may research a new market from the outside, there are inherent limitations, including language barriers and cultural nuances. An outsider's perspective can only offer so much, and without local insights, agreements with domestic partners might heavily influence foreign entrants. If these relationships sour, they can jeopardize the entire business venture.

"In the Middle East or in socialist countries, for instance, some locals place great importance on their connections with royalty or influential politicians. I've observed businesses that failed because they partnered with such individuals."

For SCL Healthcare, partnering with LX International proved invaluable for its venture in Indonesia. While SCL conducted rigorous market research, LX International, having been established in the market already, provided insights that were both richer and more practical due to their firsthand experience.

Engaging in an overseas market also exposes how other countries perceive your own. Korea's global stature has risen notably, yet there persists a certain prejudice viewing it merely as a small, divided nation in the East. Such stereotypes can be both burdensome and demoralizing in the unforgiving realm of international business. However, having a domestic partner well-acquainted with the local reality can significantly mitigate these challenges, reducing the potential impact of such prejudices.

The third crucial factor for international success involves passionate employees. Often overlooked in discussions about overseas business achievements, the enthusiasm and motivation of employees play a pivotal role in driving a venture's success.

Even the most diligent efforts by head office staff can falter if local employees, who handle day-to-day operations, do not fulfill their responsibilities. Due to the physical distance, it's challenging for the head office to monitor this directly. Therefore, it is critical that staff dispatched to the local markets are not only trustworthy but also highly capable. It is particularly vital to appoint talented and competent individuals as local leaders. The head office must provide ample support and compensation to ensure these employees can perform their duties to the best of their abilities.

The fourth factor for successful overseas expansion is sincerity. This involves showing the local communities that the company's intent goes beyond profitability; it is there to genuinely contribute to their well-being.

A company, inherently driven by its interests, cannot win the hearts of the local people if it focuses only on commercial gains. SCL Healthcare has consistently endeavored to demonstrate its commitment to improving the health and happiness of the populations in the markets it enters. This commitment was put to the test during a natural disaster in Indonesia.

While SLX employees were engaged in setting up K-LAB, a magnitude 5.6 earthquake struck the Cianjur region of West Java on November 21, 2022. Despite its moderate magnitude, the shallow epicenter of the quake led to significant devastation (334 fatalities,

8 missing persons, 44 severe injuries, 53,408 damaged houses, and approximately 114,000 people displaced. These initial figures were later revised upwards, more than doubling in most categories). Tragically, many of the victims were children.

The staff dispatched from Korea were terrified by the earthquake, an experience they had never encountered before. However, they had no time to dwell on their fears due to the urgent cries of Indonesian residents, whose homes were destroyed and families devastated in an instant. After the earthquake, heavy rain complicated rescue efforts, and ongoing aftershocks spread further fear. Outside the hospital, the desperate pleas of residents and the relentless sound of ambulance sirens intertwined.

Upon hearing the news of the Chianjur earthquake, SCL Healthcare acted swiftly to assist the victims. Recognizing the immediate need for aid, the company sent relief supplies valued at 100 million rupees (about 1.56 billion won), including blankets, tarpaulins, diapers, bottled water, and ramen.

This humanitarian response was not covered by the Korean media at the time; the priority was simply to aid those in need. A company with a mission to protect the health of the Indonesian people cannot ignore such a tragedy. Isn't this the very essence of sincerity? Companies aiming to expand overseas must carefully consider the mindset with which they approach the people of those countries.

SCL Healthcare's report card on overseas expansion is currently 'top tier'. The company is poised to take the next step, having been selected for the medical overseas expansion project support project hosted by the Korea Health Industry Development Institute. Plans are also underway to establish a Korean-style screening center in Vietnam. Looking further ahead, the company harbors even grander aspirations. Each of the Group's affiliates aims to venture into so-called advanced countries, including the United States and Europe. It's no exaggeration to say that a Korean era has dawned globally. Korean dramas, movies, music, food, and fashion are gaining international acclaim under the banner of Hallyu, the Korean Wave. Isn't it time for medicine to join this wave? Chairman Lee Kyoung Ryul is confident that K-medical will lead the global medical community within the next few years. This vision inspired the naming of the Indonesian lab as K-LAB.

While the future prospects of SCL Healthcare's overseas business endeavors remain unpredictable, certain elements will ensure its success. If the company continues to thoroughly analyze foreign markets, collaborate with domestic partners knowledgeable about local conditions, engage passionate employees, and approach international markets with sincerity, SCL Healthcare is well-positioned to realize its dreams. These four pillars of success are equally applicable to any company aspiring to thrive in the global market.

FAIL AND CHALLENGE

DEVELOPMENT OF NEW TEST METHODS

No company's history is exclusively marked by success. As previously mentioned, to err is human, and thus a history solely crafted by human hands cannot be devoid of failure. Despite this, many companies shy away from discussing their setbacks. They spotlight their successes and shroud their failures behind a veil, adhering to the misguided notion that failure equates to defeat. Yet, if you peek behind the curtain at companies celebrated for their great achievements, you'll often find a series of failures. These organizations have turned their failures into stepping stones for success by meticulously analyzing missteps and transforming them into valuable data. In this regard, failure serves as an unparalleled textbook for success. SCL Healthcare, too, has had its share of challenges and failures (or near-failures), and eventually rose above them. Here are some of those stories.

The first is associated with the company's quest to develop highly accurate prenatal tests. The dream of delivering a healthy baby is profoundly significant for expectant parents. However, with rising ages of marriage and pregnancy, coupled with increasing environmental pollution, concerns about the possibility of congenital disabilities are intensifying.

Korea stands out among OECD countries with a total fertility rate below 1, with the number of births in 2022 expected to drop below 250,000—half of what it was a decade ago. Concurrently, the incidence of high-risk pregnancies is on the rise. This decline in birth rates coupled with an increase in high-risk pregnancies has spurred growing interest in prenatal testing. Particularly, the risks associated with trisomy diseases such as Down syndrome, Edwards syndrome, and Patau syndrome have heightened the need for comprehensive fetal assessments. Medical institutions conduct various prenatal screening tests, including nuchal translucency (NT), maternal serum screening tests (MSST), non-invasive prenatal testing (NIPT), chorionic villi sampling tests (CVST), and amniotic fluid tests (AFT), relying on testing agencies like SCL for precise results.

Expectant parents face numerous challenges with prenatal genetic testing. If performed incorrectly, these tests can endanger the fetus or lead to complications. Moreover, inaccurate results can lead to failed screenings for congenital abnormalities. Consequently, medical professionals are keenly interested in screening methods that not only enhance the accuracy of detecting congenital abnormalities but also ensure the safety of both mother and fetus.

SCL has developed a test that surpasses the accuracy of both traditional invasive methods and some non-invasive tests (This development, which has been completed and reported to the Korea Disease Control and Prevention Agency, is scheduled for introduction in 2023). The test employs non-invasive prenatal genetic testing (NIPT) using Next Generation Sequencing (NGS). This innovative method can analyze even minuscule amounts of DNA, making it more sensitive and faster than existing tests. It boasts a lower false positive rate and is recognized for its heightened accuracy among non-invasive tests. Traditional tests like the nuchal translucency and maternal serum screening tests have reported false positive rates ranging from 3% to 19%. In contrast, the false positive rate for the NIPT using NGS is known to be less than 0.1%. The NIPT method developed by SCL has been verified to achieve 100% sensitivity and specificity, with a 0% rate of false positives and negatives.

In fact, the testing method developed by SCL differed significantly from previously commercialized NIPTs, presenting unique challenges in data interpretation. While established testing methods benefit from clear standards that facilitate the confirmation and analysis of results, the use of Next Generation Sequencing (NGS) required the development of new protocols. One major challenge was the separation of fetal DNA from maternal DNA (cffDNA; cell-free fetal DNA originates from the placenta and circulates in the maternal blood during pregnancy). This task is complex, and establishing and verifying bioinformatics interpretation standards for detecting chromosomal abnormalities had to be meticulously crafted from scratch.

Without existing models to guide their efforts, researchers had to navigate uncharted territory, where numerous trials and errors were inevitable. The team conducted countless sample tests, tirelessly working to perfect a reliable method for interpreting complex genetic data. Despite facing setbacks and the looming fear of failure, the dedication to their mission prevented them from giving up.

After overcoming these significant challenges, the NIPT method utilizing NGS is now on the brink of commercialization. Without the sincerity and perseverance of SCL's technology development researchers, this breakthrough in SCL's new technology would not have been possible.

There was a time when what seemed like a complete failure turned into an unexpected catalyst for growth. In 2006, the Japanese clinical testing agency LSIM proposed a multinational clinical study involving

Korea and Japan, focusing on the health indicators of smokers and non-smokers. Eager to collaborate, SCL agreed to participate alongside domestic university hospitals. However, SCL soon faced an unforeseen setback: Korean media raised ethical concerns about conducting clinical trials related to cigarettes rather than medicines. This negative publicity swayed public opinion, and as a result, Korea was unable to partake in the study (Internationally, research on smoking has consistently faced criticism—either for the mere act of studying cigarettes or due to perceived conflicts of interest influenced by multinational companies).

SCL's initial foray into international joint clinical trials seemed doomed to fail. However, the relationship and trust built with LSIM during this challenging period led to an unexpected opportunity. SCL and LSIM decided to plan a joint venture, which laid the groundwork for establishing the Standard Operating Procedures (SOP) and analysis services that now underpin C-LAB.

This venture allowed SCL to develop and operationalize C-LAB more swiftly and effectively than any other domestic specimen testing agency. The company established robust work processes and systems, ultimately gaining certification for Good Clinical Laboratory Practice (GCLP). SCL was thus reborn as a benchmark institution in the field. Had SCL been disheartened by the initial failure of the multinational clinical trial and abandoned efforts to establish the SOP, the growth and success of C-LAB might have stalled or even regressed.

Challenges encountered along the way should be viewed as opportunities to regroup and prepare for future endeavors. By using setbacks as springboards for innovation, you can open new paths to work and hope.

THE COURAGE TO FIND SUCCESS AFTER FAILURE

Post-it notes are often cited as a classic example of how a company can turn failure into substantial progress. In the 1970s, 3M researcher Spencer Silver was deeply involved in developing an adhesive that was intended to be much stronger than any existing 3M products. However, instead of creating a more powerful adhesive, he ended up with something quite different: a weak adhesive that was not very sticky, didn't dissolve, and could be removed without leaving any residue. Silver was initially puzzled by this low-tack adhesive, as it didn't stick well to anything. He presented his findings at a company seminar, but his discovery did not generate much interest. Despite this, Silver didn't give up; he continued his research, believing in the uniqueness of his creation.

A breakthrough came a few years later through an unexpected source. Arthur Fry, another 3M employee, was at church flipping through a hymnal when he encountered a problem: the paper markers he used to keep his place kept falling out. When he tried using glue to secure them, they stuck too firmly, causing frustration. It was then that he recalled the peculiar adhesive Silver had developed. Fry realized that this adhesive could be perfect for making a paper that could be easily attached to and removed from other papers without damage. Seeing the potential for a new product, Fry reported this idea back to the company.

The company's initial response was lukewarm; there was no existing data to predict whether the new product would be well-received in the market. However, the two inventors did not give up and continued their research, eventually launching what we now know as Post-it notes—originally released as a bookmark. Initially, the market's response to this innovative product was tepid. Nonetheless, the team implemented an active promotional strategy, including sending samples to companies, which eventually led to significant success. This perseverance not only paid off in terms of product success but also greatly contributed to fostering a corporate culture at 3M that embraces and learns from failures.

In 1993, Apple introduced its first portable device, the Newton. From today's vantage point, surrounded by lightweight and sleek tablets and smartphones, the Newton might seem archaic. Yet, it is considered the forerunner of the iPad and iPhone. Initially, the Newton was well-received for its innovative feature that allowed users to write or draw directly on its black-and-white LCD screen using a stylus pen. However, its success was short-lived, and it eventually faded from the market. The device struggled due to poor handwriting recognition, high costs, bulky size, and sluggish performance.

Nevertheless, the Newton, released in the early 1990s, remains a product we should remember. It is remarkable that the precursor to modern tablets and smartphones was introduced at that time. From the Newton's shortcomings, Apple learned essential lessons about what a portable device should entail. These insights helped shape the development of the iPhone and iPad, which became tremendous successes. When Steve Jobs returned to Apple in 1997, he discontinued the Newton. However, he redirected the Newton development team to focus on new projects. If Apple had been disheartened by the Newton's failure, the groundbreaking innovations of the iPhone and iPad might never have materialized.

The WD-40 Company in the United States introduced the multipurpose anti-rust lubricant 'WD-40' in 1953. This product not only lubricates but also dehumidifies and moisture-proofs metal surfaces, eliminates surface noise, and effectively cleans oil stains. Spraying it on rusty metal and wiping it off not only removes rust but also restores the metal's shine.

The origin of WD-40 is as fascinating as that of Post-it notes. It was initially developed as a corrosion inhibitor for the SM-65 Atlas, which was the first U.S. intercontinental ballistic missile (ICBM). After 39 unsuccessful attempts to perfect the formula, the 40th attempt proved successful, leading to its commercialization. The name WD-40 stands for 'Water Displacement Perfected on the 40th Try.' Initially used covertly by missile base personnel, its exceptional performance soon warranted a commercial release. Starting in a can form, it was later packaged into an aerosol can and hit retail stores in 1958.

The success of WD-40 spurred rapid growth for the company, which was eventually renamed after the product due to its popularity. In the early 1960s, WD-40 was used to repair flood-damaged vehicles and machinery during a major flood in Texas, and during the Vietnam War, it was employed by the military to fix rusted weapons. Today, WD-40 is a household staple, found in nearly every home and used in over 160 countries, including Korea, in any setting that involves metal materials.

The fact that it took 40 attempts to develop WD-40 is a testament to the great perseverance of the company's team. Had founder Norman Larsen and his staff given up after 39 failures, WD-40 would never have come into existence. The success of the 40th trial rendered the previous 39 attempts both meaningful and rewarding.

Nintendo, a leading video game manufacturer in Japan, was

established in 1889. Originally a playing card company, it achieved success in 1953 by producing the world's first plastic playing cards. Despite various subsequent business ventures that failed and led to a decline, Nintendo shifted its focus to toy manufacturing and, in 1977, began making electronic video game consoles.

In 1980, Nintendo of America was established, and the company exported a game called 'Radar Scope' to the United States. Initially, the response was underwhelming, and the business was unprofitable. However, Nintendo made a miraculous comeback with the release of the video game "Donkey Kong," which not only cleared their unsold inventory but also turned their sales around. The 1985 launch of the "Super Mario" series marked a major success. Today, Nintendo is a global video game powerhouse with a massive fan base. Had Nintendo not persevered through its early challenges in the US market, it would not have evolved into the video game giant it is today.

Many people have a habit of hiding their failures, pretending they never occurred. Humans are not perfect, yet often strive to appear flawless, driven by a fear of failure.

This fear stems from the belief that failure negates all effort, resources, and time invested. More profoundly, it brands us as 'failures.' Accepting failure without fear is not as easy as it may seem, and overcoming this sense of defeat requires transforming failure into a living experience.

Discussing failure openly is essential because it is a necessary passage on the path to success. The companies mentioned earlier succeeded because they used failure as a springboard for innovation. They saw failure not as a setback but as a direction unconsidered before, a door to new opportunities, and a catalyst for innovation.

A company must tolerate its employees' failures. If failures are met with disdain and people are penalized for them, nobody will dare to propose creative ideas. Instead, employees should be encouraged to make attempts, record them, analyze the results, and seek better directions. These attempts, whether successful or not, are inherently meaningful. Successes should be developed further, and failures should be dissected to understand what improvements are needed, focusing on processes, resource allocations, and decision-making.

American broadcaster Oprah Winfrey once said, "Failure is defined by how we deal with failure." Indeed, the true measure of failure is determined by the actions that follow. By not dwelling on setbacks and instead planning for future endeavors, the entire landscape can shift dramatically. Ultimately, it is up to the individual whether they will rise to shining success or remain subdued by failure.

A SENSE OF MISSION FOR
SCIENTIFIC DATA

TWO PHRASES THAT MADE RESEARCHERS
NERVOUS

You might recall learning about the 'mitochondrion' from your school science textbooks. Mitochondria are organelles within cells that play a crucial role in cellular respiration, the process that generates energy within cells. Essentially, they act as energy-producing factories and are involved in various cellular functions including the cell cycle, cell differentiation, cell death, and signal transmission. They consist of a double membrane structure with inner and outer layers, and the convoluted inner membrane houses mitochondrial-specific DNA, rRNA, and tRNA.

The SCL Companion Biomarker (CB) Center received a request from Professor L of I Medical University Hospital for genetic analysis.

For ten years, Professor L had been studying cases of damage caused by humidifier disinfectants and requested analysis of mitochondrial nucleic acids in the cells of the victims. The phrases 'humidifier disinfectant victims' and 'mitochondrial nucleic acid analysis' were enough to unsettle the researchers at the CB Center. The humidifier disinfectant incident, considered one of the worst social disasters in Korea, involved a large number of casualties due to products containing harmful chemicals. These products were exclusive to Korea, with no similar cases reported in other countries.

The issue first emerged in the mid-1990s when patients began presenting with unexplained lung diseases each spring. The severity of the issue was acknowledged in the mid-2000s, and although the medical community alerted the government, a thorough investigation was not conducted immediately. It wasn't until 2011 that an epidemiological investigation finally linked the mysterious lung diseases to the toxic chemicals in humidifier disinfectants, leading to national shock and outrage.

Among the ingredients of humidifier disinfectants, polyhexamethylene guanidine phosphate (PHMG-P) is particularly problematic. It has been shown to cause fatal lung damage when inhaled by animals. The academic community has also emphasized the need to study the toxicity of chloromethylisothiazolinone (CMIT) and methylisothiazolinone (MIT), alongside PHMG-P, to understand their links to lung diseases.

Professor L selected three families from the affected victims to analyze their nucleic acids, aiming to detect any mitochondrial mutations. This investigation was prompted by the symptoms exhibited by the victims, who suffered from chronic fatigue syndrome in addition to severe lung diseases such as heart failure, respiratory failure, and pulmonary fibrosis. Their prolonged, severe fatigue led Professor L to suspect a mitochondrial abnormality, considering mitochondria are known as the energy factories of the body.

To explore this further, Professor L drew blood from the subjects, conducted cell fluorescent staining, and examined the mitochondrial membrane. He observed that the mitochondria's shape differed from that of normal mitochondria. Most notably, Professor L hypothesized that a mutation might have occurred at the germline level, evidenced by a victim who had given birth to a child post-exposure. The child also exhibited symptoms similar to those affected by the disinfectants. Consequently, Professor L requested a mitochondrial mutation test from SCL, specifically using Next Generation Sequencing (NGS) to identify any genetic mutations.

But there was a problem: the SCL CB Center had never isolated mitochondria from cells before. Although SCL was among the few institutions in Korea capable of conducting NGS analysis (next-generation sequencing analysis that involves fragmenting a single genome into numerous pieces and then assembling the base sequences by computer to analyze the genome information), the company had not analyzed mitochondria alone.

Isolating mitochondria from blood cells presented a formidable technical hurdle. Nonetheless, the researchers were committed to overcoming it. They scoured a vast array of academic papers to find a viable method for mitochondrial separation and conducted numerous experiments. Given the context—this request stemmed from a case involving numerous victims still embroiled in legal disputes, with many lives lost and survivors in ongoing pain—the team approached their work with an intensified sense of mission.

The results were startling. They identified a mitochondrial mutation unique to the victims, which seemed to be linked to the humidifier disinfectant exposure. The mitochondrial membranes were riddled with holes, a significant abnormality clearly distinguishable from those in the control group. Equally surprising was the hereditary nature of this mutation. Among victims who had been single at the time of exposure but later married and had children, similar mitochondrial deformities were observed in their offspring.

The mechanism by which the toxic chemicals in humidifier disinfectants caused mitochondrial mutations is still under investigation. However, it has been confirmed that such mutations do occur. These findings were relayed to Professor L, who is actively working to raise awareness about the adverse effects of humidifier disinfectants on human health and the suffering of the victims. Ongoing research suggests that mitochondrial abnormalities are closely linked to the development of serious health conditions such as diabetes, metabolic syndrome, Alzheimer's disease, and Parkinson's disease (according to the Humidifier Disinfectant Symposium held in July 2021).

THE CULPRIT THAT DISAPPEARED INTO THIN AIR

The media often referred to the humidifier disinfectant damage incident as the case of the "culprit that disappeared into thin air." As of January 31, 2023, a total of 7,811 damage reports had been filed, including 200 withdrawals, with the number of deaths attributed to pulmonary fibrosis reaching 1,802, according to the Humidifier Disinfectant Damage Support Comprehensive Portal. Given that the products were launched in 1994 and the cause was not identified until 2011, it is likely that many more victims remain uncounted.

Medical experts who have studied cases of humidifier disinfectant damage report that the harm extends beyond the lungs, affecting the entire body. Currently, 6,009 individuals are suffering from various diseases related to exposure, including lung disease, skin conditions, chronic fatigue, mental illnesses, and ADHD. However, the diseases officially recognized by the government as related to humidifier disinfectants are limited to 10 categories, including lung disease, asthma, fetal damage, toxic hepatitis, interstitial lung disease in both children and adults, bronchiectasis, pneumonia, bronchitis, and upper respiratory diseases.

In 1994, when the advertisement for "The World's First Humidifier Disinfectants Released" was widely circulated, no one could have foreseen the ensuing catastrophe. As the public grappled with fear over an unidentified "disease," the government's lack of response exacerbated the situation. It was alarming that none of the companies that introduced these humidifier disinfectants, including the very first company to launch them, adequately investigated the toxicity of the chemical ingredients to human health. Although tests on the ingredients were commissioned, the products were released before the results were available. The products even carried the KC mark, and advertisements reassured consumers of their harmlessness to humans. The suffering of the victims continues to worsen due to the lack of adequate punishment for those responsible for manufacturing and distributing these harmful products and the absence of proper compensation for the victims. Only four individuals, including the former CEO of Company "O" that used the PHMG-P ingredient, have been sentenced to prison. On January 12, 2021, the first trial court acquitted all 13 executives and employees of the company, finding them not guilty of negligent homicide on the grounds that a causal link between the chemicals CMIT/MIT and lung disease could not be established. In April 2022, seven companies agreed to a damage relief mediation plan proposed by the Humidifier Disinfectant Damage Relief Adjustment Committee, but Company "O" and Company "A" rejected it. The resolution of this case and justice for the victims remain uncertain.

In June 2021, a collection of essays titled *My Body is the Evidence* was published, documenting the harrowing experiences of 63 individuals from 25 families who suffered due to humidifier disinfectants. These narratives vividly describe the extensive physical, mental, and economic hardships endured by the victims. As media highlights, the "culprit" has disappeared into thin air, leaving countless victims to suffer profound agony.

It has been 29 years since humidifier disinfectants were first introduced to the market, and 12 years since it was discovered that toxic ingredients in these products were the cause of mysterious lung diseases. This disaster starkly illustrates the consequences of governmental negligence and the irresponsibility of manufacturers who used harmful ingredients. Such tragedies must never be allowed to occur again.

Regardless of technological advancements, the true value of technology lies in its ethical application. Developers and researchers must recognize that their work can either illuminate the world or cause indiscriminate harm.

The humidifier disinfectant incident serves as a critical reminder for researchers to reflect on their approach to product development, efficacy, and side effect research. Amid a decade-long battle over accountability, suspicions have arisen about some individuals who may have sided with the manufacturers, covertly profited, manipulated research outcomes, or disregarded the harmful effects of their products. These unethical practices are reprehensible and must be vehemently condemned. Human life should invariably be the foremost priority. Developers who create products and researchers who evaluate their effects must fully comprehend the significance of their work. Companies must not pressure their employees to sacrifice safety for profit. As the sway of capital intensifies, it demands a corresponding rise in chaos, highlighting the urgent need for integrity in scientific research and product development.

SCL conducted an objective and fair test upon request from a professor who had been dedicated to raising public awareness about the dangers of humidifier disinfectant damage. Despite the high level of technical expertise required and potential repercussions from powerful, wealthy companies, the committed team of experts at SCL did not shy away from the challenge. Their ability to proceed was driven by a profound sense of mission to produce unbiased scientific data, regardless of the requester. SCL was the pioneer in Korea to

159

perform mitochondrial nucleic acid tests on victims of humidifier disinfectant exposure. The successful production of these test results was not only a testament to SCL's capabilities but also a somber reflection on the victims' ongoing suffering. The incident underscores a crucial principle: no compromise should be made when human life is at stake.

Regardless of technological advancements, the true value of technology lies in its ethical application. Developers and researchers must recognize that their work can either illuminate the world or cause indiscriminate harm. Winston Churchill once remarked, "A compromiser is like someone who feeds crocodiles knowing that they will be eaten by them in the end." This serves as a cautionary tale for those who prioritize market dominance over ethics. Ultimately, those who compromise on ethics may enjoy temporary success, but they will inevitably face the consequences of the very dangers they have enabled.

Chapter **4**

DIAMONDS PULLED
OUT OF THE MUD

When everyone is stuck in the mud, complaining and resenting,
someone pulls a diamond out of it.
Rather than blaming the crisis, try to overcome it.
Then you will seize the opportunity that shines like a diamond.

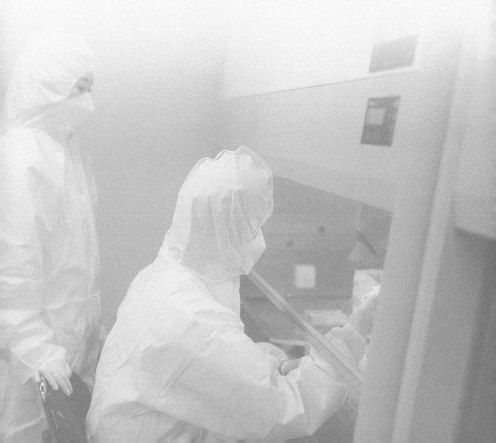

OVERCOMING
THE COVID-19 TSUNAMI

THE SCARIEST WORDS IN THE WORLD

"Team Leader, do you have a moment?"

Not again, thought the molecular diagnostics team leader when the employee asked that question. He almost froze, as if someone had pressed the pause button. Please, don't let me hear what I dread to hear, he thought. He had to somehow get out of this situation. What should I say? All sorts of thoughts were racing through his head.

"Oh, I'm sorry. I don't have time right now..."

"Please give me a moment. I really need to tell you something."

The employee started walking ahead of the team leader. The determination in the employee's footsteps was evident. The team leader knew he could not avoid it. He had no choice but to follow. The two sat across from each other at a table in a corner of the lab.

"Team Leader, I'll work until the end of this month and then resign. You've been so supportive, and I'm grateful for that... I'm sorry."

It was the announcement he had dreaded. The team leader closed his eyes tightly. So, this is how I lose another team member, he thought. Many team members had left the company since the coronavirus pandemic began. This employee must have been overwhelmed by the constant overnight and overtime work as the number of tests skyrocketed. The team leader asked him to stay at least two weeks longer than planned because it was a desperate time, and thankfully, he agreed to stay another month. The team leader felt bittersweet as he watched the employee's back as he returned to his seat.

What should I write in the job posting? SCL had been posting job openings almost every month. I wondered if there had ever been this many postings since the company was founded. Should I include that the job involves conducting coronavirus tests, or should I omit it? I agonized over whether I could really hire someone if I was honest about the current demands. His mind was a whirl of confusion.

All team members were fully committed, pouring their hearts and strength into their work, but this team member stood out particularly. He took care of his juniors and was considerate of his seniors. The team leader was well aware of his dedication and effort. Losing him was devastating, yet he couldn't stop him from leaving. It was just as painful as when other team members had resigned—they all loved their work and took pride in being part of SCL.

The COVID-19 pandemic brought many challenges, but staffing issues were particularly troublesome. "I think about 50% of the employees quit because they couldn't endure it," the molecular diagnostics team leader recalled.

COVID specimens arrived like a tsunami. They kept coming in like relentless waves crashing against the shore. It was impossible to predict the volume of specimens for the next day. The seemingly endless influx was what frightened the molecular diagnostics team the most.

Employees sacrificed their holidays, tirelessly handling the surging number of test samples. Despite many being highly experienced, the relentless pace of working 6-7 days a week became physically unbearable. The team leader himself noted, "There was a time when I only took one day off a month." That's why he couldn't fault those who chose to leave. As the virus spread, the number of employees contracting it increased. With staff members resigning or falling ill, the burden on the remaining employees grew heavier.

Historically, our ancestors feared tigers and smallpox most, but for the inspection team leaders, the most dreaded moment was when a team member approached to say, "Do you have a moment?" That phrase alone was enough to make everyone tense.

PEOPLE WHO FOUGHT AGAINST
THE GOD OF DEATH

The first confirmed case of COVID-19 in Korea was reported on January 21, 2020. Initially, the situation seemed manageable. Having learned from the MERS outbreak in 2015, the Korea Centers for Disease Control and Prevention (now the Korea Disease Control and Prevention Agency) had established comprehensive guidelines for handling large-scale infectious diseases. These included quarantine of confirmed cases, temporary lockdowns of outbreak sites, epidemiological investigations, and isolation and testing of contacts. Consequently, authorities quickly began proactive measures to identify and manage suspected cases following the early COVID-19 detections. However, by late February 2020, the situation dramatically worsened. It escalated notably following the 31st confirmed case on February 18, an individual who had attended a large religious gathering, sparking a significant outbreak. The daily testing numbers soared from around 1,000 to several thousand a day, eventually surpassing 10,000 by 2021. The public atmosphere shifted drastically as fear took hold, driven by the rapid spread of this little-understood contagious disease. In China, televised scenes depicted people hammering nails into the doors of homes with confirmed cases to prevent movement. As reports of severe illnesses and deaths from COVID-19 proliferated across media outlets worldwide, including in Korea, public anxiety peaked. This palpable fear led people to queue at pharmacies daily to purchase masks, while streets, restaurants, and shopping malls became eerily deserted due to the sharp decline in foot traffic.

The medical field was akin to a battlefield: The number of confirmed cases skyrocketed, leading to a severe shortage of hospital beds, which also adversely affected the treatment of other seriously ill patients. The virus spread within hospital settings as well, necessitating the isolation of medical staff and exacerbating the already critical workforce shortage. Medical staff felt as if they were perpetually on the brink, pushed to their limits every day.

Despite the intense situation on the ground, there were no detailed strategies in place for securing quarantine supplies, testing tools, equipment, assigning personnel to screening clinics, or establishing quarantine guidelines and support measures for medical institutions. The severity of the surge had been unforeseen, catching everyone off guard. Medical staff courageously dove into the fray, while medical institutions and testing agencies made enormous sacrifices, battling valiantly in this all-out war against the virus. Without their unwavering dedication, the COVID-19 situation would have spiraled into an even more dire crisis.

An emergency was declared across all departments at SCL. Normally, the SCL molecular diagnostic team could handle around 500 tests

One of the many challenges faced by the molecular diagnostic team in the early stages of the pandemic was the lack of information about the novel virus known as 'COVID-19'. Unlike usual pathogens, which were well-documented, COVID-19 was a new type of virus, previously unknown and unstudied.

per day with their existing personnel. Each day, team members would prepare by checking testing equipment and tools, receiving results from the previous day's tests, and then conducting the day's scheduled tests, later entering the results into the computer. However, after the outbreak of COVID-19, this routine and methodical work system completely collapsed.

In the early stages of the outbreak, an astounding 3,000 to 4,000 specimens were arriving daily. The sheer volume was not just overwhelming in terms of numbers; the logistical challenges it presented were unprecedented. Screening centers at public health facilities nationwide were pushed to the brink, experiencing a level of chaos that led to mental breakdowns among staff and resulted in improper recording of specimens and test records. Team members were forced to start from scratch, painstakingly comparing the notations on specimens with the information on test records and making corrections as necessary.

The normal rotation between day and night shifts became unsustainable. Personnel assigned to day shifts were also required at night, and those scheduled for night shifts found themselves working during the day. They worked for eight hours straight, rested briefly in their dorms, then returned to continue handling the ever-increasing influx of specimens.

Meanwhile, a fierce competition erupted among testing agencies to secure the necessary testing tools and equipment. Responding to COVID-19 was a race against time. The most daunting task was to quickly amass enough testing equipment, tools, and personnel to manage the surge in test samples. When an infectious disease strikes, the Korea Centers for Disease Control and Prevention (KCDC) issues a crisis alert with four stages: 'Attention　Caution　Alert　Serious.' The Central Disaster and Safety Countermeasures Headquarters is activated from stage 2, 'Caution.' At stage 4, 'Serious,' a pan-governmental, all-out response system is implemented, which was necessitated on February 23, 2020, as the virus began to spread rapidly. The escalation was so sudden that it did not allow for gradual preparation over time; thus, SCL and other testing agencies were not fully prepared with the necessary materials internally. This situation mirrored the challenges faced across the sector.

SCL urgently contacted pharmaceutical companies to order the reagents and equipment needed for testing. Caught off guard by the sudden onslaught of COVID-19, these companies struggled to fulfill the surge in orders, causing considerable frustration. Securing supplies quickly became a critical priority for testing agencies. At SCL, nearly every department mobilized to assist. While the administrative department handled most orders, members of the testing departments, including the molecular diagnostics team, reached out to contacts at pharmaceutical companies, imploring them through pleas, coaxing, and urgent requests for expedited help.

One of the many challenges faced by the molecular diagnostic team in the early stages of the pandemic was the lack of information about the novel virus known as 'COVID-19'. Unlike usual pathogens, which were well-documented, COVID-19 was a new type of virus, previously unknown and unstudied. It was shrouded in uncertainty like a dense fog. As data slowly accumulated, the team grappled with learning about the virus while managing the fear of infection themselves. Despite the risks, they donned protective gear and diligently analyzed samples, driven by the imperative to combat this lethal threat and save lives.

Performing PCR tests, specifically 'reverse transcription polymerase chain reaction (RT-PCR)', required Level D protective clothing, akin to hooded onesies for infants but for adults. The process of suiting up was meticulous: disinfect hands, don inner gloves, put on surgical clothing, then the protective suit, and overshoes. Next, an N95 mask and goggles were added, followed by a hood, and finally, outer gloves. It took over 10 minutes just to put on the protective gear.

Imagine working for over 10 hours wrapped in layers like this. Even with clothing designed to absorb and release sweat efficiently, and even in a strongly air-conditioned room, the sweat was relentless.

Scrubs were worn under the protective suit primarily to manage this excessive sweating.

Even a simple task like going to the bathroom became a formidable challenge. Every bathroom break required removing and then redoning the protective suit, followed by a thorough washing process. If there was any suspicion of contamination, a completely new suit was necessary. Due to the inconvenience and time lost, the bathroom became a dreaded destination. It was common for team members to suppress the urge to go for five or six hours, which eventually extended to nine or ten hours. Each day, they seemed to break their own endurance records.

They even shared strategies to minimize bathroom visits, such as avoiding water intake, fasting for about 12 hours, or substituting meals with candy. Although the company provided meals in shifts and offered snacks, team members often relinquished their basic needs—eating, sleeping, and using the restroom—focused on the urgent task of delivering test results to anxious individuals awaiting news. Thus, asking, "How many hours since you've been to the bathroom?" became a form of self-discipline for the molecular diagnostic team during the pandemic.

THE POWER TO PERSEVERE THROUGH PAINFUL TIMES

In the initial days of the COVID-19 outbreak, the SCL molecular diagnostic team responsible for COVID-19 testing did not go home. It was because they were overwhelmed with work, and also because they felt it was irresponsible to return to their families. The full nature of the new virus was still unknown, mirroring the early days of MERS and the new influenza, where even experts faced significant fear regarding the infectious disease. Opting for self-isolation, they chose to stay away from home to avoid potentially exposing their families to the virus.

In consideration of their employees' sacrifices, the company provided accommodations close to the lab, allowing them to maintain contact with their families primarily through phone calls. When asked about their health, whether they had eaten, or if they had been infected, they would uniformly respond with, "I'm fine." The primary concern for these team members was not for themselves but for their families' well-being. Reflecting on that time, the team leader shared, "My wife was the only person I told that I was conducting COVID-19 tests. I instructed her never to disclose what I was doing to anyone else, because I was afraid that people might shun her as if they had seen a bomb."

The social atmosphere was exceedingly tense as COVID-19 spread. Initially, the policy required isolating both confirmed cases and those in close contact, leading to heightened neighborhood anxiety whenever ambulances arrived or individuals in protective suits were seen. Infected individuals were subjected to harsh stares, almost as if they were criminals. Online rumors frequently exacerbated fears, claiming that numerous infections had occurred in specific locations due to a few confirmed cases. Those labeled as super spreaders were sometimes outed by the so-called 'Netizen Investigation Squad'. As the saying goes, 'If you get caught, you die', suggesting that society was searching for scapegoats to blame for the public health crisis.

In this climate of suspicion and fear, all SCL employees felt compelled to conceal their roles, moving through their communities with the secrecy of those hiding from wrongdoing, even though they didn't do anything wrong.

Now, with testing equipment and personnel fully in place, results are available within 4 hours. However, in the early days of the pandemic, obtaining test results could take anywhere from 8 to 12 hours. As anxiety mounted, many people eagerly pressed public health centers and hospitals for quicker responses. Some, unable to wait, even contacted SCL directly after pestering public health center staff.

Public inquiries about COVID-19 tests generally fell into two categories: those impatient for results and those who outright denied their positive results.

"I need to get surgery soon. What's taking so long?"

"I'm positive for COVID-19? Stop talking nonsense!"

In cases where individuals sought faster results, SCL staff would explain calmly that results had to be obtained through the appropriate public health center or hospital. Due to the Personal Information Protection Act, disclosing patient information without proper verification is illegal. It's not just any information; it's the patient's personal information. No institution would hand it over simply because someone claims to be the guardian of the tested individual. Even if the person being tested makes contact in person, confirming their identity is challenging and sharing information without proper verification is a violation of regulations. Therefore, regardless of how upset the person on the other end of the phone might be, SCL had no choice but to inform them, "You need to obtain the results from the hospital or public health center."

The latter is much more of a headache than the former.

The situations involving denial of positive results were particularly complex. For instance, a nursing assistant might protest being mistakenly labeled as a spreader at work, understandable given the societal stigma at the time. Despite empathizing with their distress, SCL staff could not disregard scientific facts. When a test subject, convinced of their negative status, demanded a retest after an explosive reaction, it only added to the physical exhaustion and mental strain faced by the testing staff. Despite these challenges, the staff at SCL empathized deeply with each test subject's difficult circumstances, silently hoping they would find the strength to navigate through these turbulent times.

TYPES OF PCR TEST RESULTS THAT TROUBLE PEOPLE

A genetic nucleic acid test is utilized to detect COVID-19 virus infection. Globally, the specific gene segments tested can vary, but in Korea, the PCR test targets three specific genes: the E gene, the RdRp segment of the ORF1b gene, and the N gene. To collect a sample, a swab is inserted into the nasopharynx and oropharynx, RNA is extracted, and then amplified to check for these genes. Typically, the test result is either negative or positive. However, the progression from testing positive to recovery and eventually testing negative can vary greatly among individuals. Some may test negative immediately, while others might continue to test positive for the virus in their body even when it is no longer infectious, necessitating ongoing testing until a negative result is achieved.

The test result can also depend on the number of amplifications performed during the PCR process. While the exact number of amplifications can vary depending on the testing reagents used, it generally ranges between 30 and 40 cycles. The fewer the cycles required to detect the virus, the higher the viral load in the sample. For instance, a positive result at 30 cycles indicates a clear presence of the virus, but a result that turns positive only after 34 cycles may be considered ambiguous. In such cases, a re-examination is necessary. If remaining samples are available, they are reanalyzed; if not, a new sample must be collected from the individual.

Occasionally, a coronavirus test may yield an 'Inconclusive' result instead of a straightforward positive or negative. This occurs when the test result hovers right on the borderline—the cut-off line—between negative and positive. Such results can indicate an early-stage infection or the presence of 'Fragment Virus' in individuals who may not be aware they are infected.

Many infectious disease specialists note that an 'inconclusive' result can occur when a person is asymptomatic, undergoes natural recovery, but traces of the virus remain in the body. These traces, referred to as 'viral residue,' are non-contagious. Even post-recovery, individuals who have been previously diagnosed with COVID-19 may receive an 'inconclusive' result during a PCR test due to this residual viral presence. When an ambiguous 'inconclusive' result is received, it necessitates a retest, often leading to complaints and concerns from the tested individual about whether they need to self-quarantine, despite exhibiting no symptoms. This situation presents challenges for both the tester and the tested individual.

False negatives, where the test results are negative despite the person being infected, and false positives, where the results are positive when the individual is actually negative, are also problematic. The introduction of self-diagnosis kits in early 2022 led to an increase in false negatives for COVID-19. As the number of confirmed cases surged, screening clinics became overwhelmed. Consequently, the government required individuals to first use a self-diagnosis kit and only seek a PCR or rapid antigen test if that result was positive. However, criticism arose due to the low accuracy of these kits (around 60% on average), attributed to errors in sample collection and testing by users. These inaccuracies, particularly the false negatives, were linked to a significant spread of COVID-19, as infected individuals unknowingly continued their daily activities, contributing to the fourth wave of the pandemic.

The issue of false positives is often attributed to contamination of the sample, reagent, or testing equipment during handling. Despite thorough cleaning, contamination in genetic amplification equipment from previous tests can lead to the detection of the virus due to the equipment's high sensitivity. This scenario underscores the importance of rigorous standards in sample handling and equipment maintenance to ensure the accuracy of test results.

To effectively control the coronavirus, it's crucial to minimize the likelihood of uncertain or incorrect test results. As new viruses like the coronavirus can emerge at any time, learning from our current experiences and enhancing testing methods is vital. By doing so, we can be better prepared to handle similar challenges in the future.

A SENSE OF MISSION FOR LIFE

Despite facing numerous challenges, SCL employees consistently adhered to their duties of testing samples. They expressed a common sentiment: "I can't say I did it because I wanted to. I am also a human being; there are times when I am afraid and reluctant. But it is something I chose to do. Someone has to do it."

The employees shared that without their deep sense of mission, enduring the difficult times would have been nearly impossible. So, what exactly is this sense of mission that empowers them to overcome such challenges? A sense of mission can be defined as a mindset committed to performing a given task well. To fulfill a mission effectively, one must understand the reasons behind it—the value of the work. Those with a strong sense of mission recognize the importance of their tasks and are willing to undertake them, even when it's tough or puts their own well-being at risk.

It is widely recognized in corporate management that high salaries and generous welfare benefits can boost employee motivation, but these factors alone are insufficient. This is because humans inherently seek to pursue values beyond material gains. Abraham Harold Maslow, an American philosopher and psychologist, illustrated this through his five-stage theory of needs, which culminates in 'self-actualization.' According to Maslow, the hierarchy progresses from physiological needs, to safety, belonging and affection, esteem, and finally, self-actualization.

When employees overcome challenges with a sense of mission and successfully complete their tasks, they fulfill their self-actualization needs. This fulfillment not only satisfies them on a deeper level but also inspires them to dream bigger and strive harder, facilitating continuous personal and professional growth.

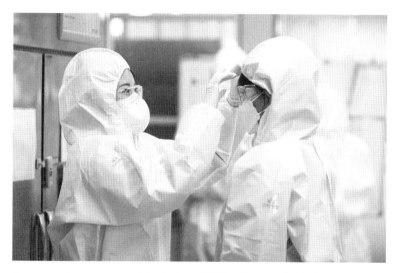

As reports of severe cases and deaths from COVID-19 increased globally, the molecular diagnostic team members were understandably apprehensive about infection. Nevertheless, they donned their protective gear and labored tirelessly, day and night, to analyze samples. They recognized that confronting this formidable challenge was essential—their relentless effort was the only way to combat the spread of the virus, a fight against the god of death to save lives.

Conversely, without self-actualization, work becomes unfulfilling, leading to disengagement and eventual departure from the organization. This underscores why leading companies must articulate a clear vision and direction for their work, inspiring employees with a sense of mission.

A strong sense of mission not only anchors employees to their company but also maximizes their potential. It encourages perseverance through difficult tasks, fosters innovative thinking, and promotes unity among colleagues. It also enhances their connection to the community, motivating them to make meaningful contributions.

That's how Team SCL was able to persevere. Overcoming the COVID-19 crisis was possible thanks to the tireless efforts of these dedicated employees. Conditions have improved significantly since the height of the pandemic. The situation has stabilized, public understanding of COVID-19 has grown, and SCL has amassed considerable expertise through the ordeal.

No matter how daunting or painful the moment, a strong sense of mission can provide the endurance needed. For SCL employees, it was this profound sense of commitment to preserving life that bolstered them through the toughest times. When a company successfully fosters a sense of mission among its workforce, employees are inspired to do whatever it takes to fulfill their roles. This dedication not only satisfies their desire for self-actualization but also drives the company's growth and development.

ANTS CARRYING A MORTAR

FROM BAD TO WORSE

In late January 2020, the COVID-19 virus landed in Korea from China and spread rapidly, leading to a nationwide mask shortage. Masks were crucial for curbing the spread of the virus, but the pace of the outbreak outstripped the existing production capabilities. China, responsible for approximately 50% of the world's mask production, ceased exports to meet its own skyrocketing domestic needs. This scenario was mirrored by major countries like the United States and Europe, each halting exports to prioritize their own demands, culminating in a global mask shortage.

Citizens lined up for hours at pharmacies to purchase masks. Prices surged to two to three times the usual rates, with some masks costing over ₩4,000 each. Despite being willing to pay a premium, people often returned home empty-handed, deepening the panic in a situation where the disease's characteristics were still largely unknown.

Employees responsible for procuring medical supplies and equipment felt the pressure intensely. With the testing department operating around the clock to manage the deluge of samples, masks were critical to maintaining safety protocols. At the onset of the pandemic, KF94 masks were not as readily available as they are today. Initially, dental masks and N95 masks, typically used for tuberculosis testing, were prioritized for departments at the highest risk of infection. Securing a steady supply of KF94 masks for frontline workers quickly became a top priority.

"It felt like being on an actual battlefield. We faced supply challenges during the 2009 swine flu and the 2015 MERS outbreaks, but nothing compared to this."

If even a single item required for testing is missing, the entire testing process grinds to a halt. Approximately 100 different types of equipment and supplies are essential for conducting testing. A shortage of even a single item could bring the entire testing process to a standstill. Driven by this urgency, the purchasing department staff worked tirelessly. They projected the necessary quantities for the upcoming three months, considering the number of employees, to prevent any disruptions in the testing process. This involved reaching out directly to mask manufacturers and factories to ensure sufficient stock was secured.

Securing Level D protective clothing proved particularly challenging. When reports of the COVID-19 virus first emerged from Wuhan, Hubei Province, China in November 2019, SCL had preemptively purchased protective gear. However, as the situation deteriorated rapidly, the initial stockpile proved inadequate. Initially, they managed with the supplies they had on hand, but soon they were scouring the internet, buying pieces wherever they could find them. The cost of protective clothing tripled, and as the number of testers needing it increased, the financial burden became significant. Negotiating reasonable prices with suppliers while meeting the inspection department's needs was a constant struggle.

Securing reagents and equipment was equally fraught. In February 2020, the Ministry of Food and Drug Safety approved the emergency use of four diagnostic reagents. New reagents continued to be released thereafter. Even with the official approval, each reagent required an internal evaluation to ensure there were no issues with its use in testing. This evaluation process added another layer of complexity to the already challenging task of securing adequate supplies.

SCL relied on equipment from a multinational medical and pharmaceutical company based in Switzerland. During the pandemic, when securing equipment became a challenge, finding replacements for current equipment became a top priority. SCL focused on acquiring models capable of testing multiple samples simultaneously, which were newly released. As the pandemic progressed, both domestic and international pharmaceutical companies and medical device manufacturers rapidly began producing related products. SCL employees proactively monitored the development of new reagents and equipment, sought substitutes for current supplies, and made concerted efforts to prevent any interruptions in testing. They kept abreast of supply and demand situations not only in Korea but also in key international markets like the US, China, and India.

Even with a three-month supply secured based on the current number of testing personnel, a sudden increase in staff the next day due to rising testing demands meant that supplies had to be reassessed and replenished to accommodate the expanded team. Managing these variables was among the most challenging aspects.

"Like all departments at SCL, the purchasing department operated seven days a week. There's a status board in the testing room for communication. When testing personnel jot down the supplies they need, the support department staff personally visit to check and procure them in advance. This proactive approach is meant to streamline operations, allowing us to respond swiftly to the testing department's needs before a formal request is made."

Despite sometimes securing a three-month supply of essential items, these reserves would often deplete within just a week. Employees tirelessly mobilized every available method to ensure that the testing process was not hindered by a lack of supplies. They engaged in daily negotiations, fighting and pleading with suppliers to meet their urgent needs.

On March 5, 2020, in response to escalating difficulties, the government implemented a supply and demand stabilization measure known as the "5-day mask rotation system." To increase the accessibility of masks, the government stipulated that the purchase of masks would be based on the last digit of the year of birth, designating specific days for each group. Additionally, the price of masks, which had skyrocketed up to tenfold, was capped at 1,500, and the number of public masks purchasable per person was limited to two. Beyond these, individuals were allowed to purchase up to five non-public masks each. This system, which lasted nearly three months, gradually eased the mask crisis.

When asked to describe that period in a single phrase, purchasing department employees said it was a time of going "from bad to worse." Each resolved issue—be it masks, reagents, equipment, or other supplies—seemed to be immediately replaced by another. Even after a long day's work, as they lay down to rest, they were plagued with anxiety over the uncertainties that the next day might bring. They endured some of the coldest and harshest times in a period that was difficult for everyone.

LEANING ON EACH OTHER

As the number of confirmed COVID-19 cases surged, the influx of calls inquiring about test results and requests for expedited processing persisted until dawn. As a testing agency in the midst of a global crisis, SCL had no choice but to respond diligently.

The COVID-19 pandemic necessitated a 24-hour emergency work system across all departments at SCL. Not only the testing department, but also the administration and sales departments were on constant alert. The sales team, in particular, often collected COVID-19 samples until the early hours of the morning at the request of hospitals and public health centers, ensuring timely delivery to the testing department. They would set alarms for brief naps and remain on standby through the night. As soon as results became available, they communicated them to public health centers and other relevant organizations.

Public health centers nationwide also operated 24-hour situation rooms, prompting SCL to organize thrice-daily sample collections—during the day, evening, and night. Emergency testing requests were handled immediately, regardless of the time. The first batch of samples, collected in the morning, was tested and results were delivered by the afternoon. The second batch, collected in the afternoon, was processed overnight with results communicated early the next morning. The third batch, collected in the evening, was tested overnight, with results reported by 6 a.m. This rigorous schedule ensured that testing and results delivery were conducted in real-time.

"The intensity of nighttime work during the pandemic is incomparable to any emergency transport operations we've handled before."

The employees of the medical diagnosis division, who were responsible for delivering COVID-19 samples, along with those at the national customer support center, faced daily overtime due to the rapidly increasing number of confirmed cases. Despite additional staffing, the workload necessitated significantly longer hours. It was common for staff to collect samples from regional bases and transport them directly to the main office, often arriving early in the morning, staying overnight, and then returning to their regional offices. Days off during weekends and holidays became a distant memory.

"In the beginning, there was widespread fear due to the unknown nature of the virus. All testing procedures had to be expedited to alleviate the public's fear of death, leaving no room for delays in our response."

Handling COVID-19 test samples added a profound sense of fear and urgency to their tasks. Employees took extra precautions, sealing the samples securely, boxing them, and marking each with a distinctive sticker indicating the need for careful handling. Despite their expertise, the palpable risk of handling an unknown infectious disease caused understandable anxiety among the staff.

The testing department, at times dealing with tens of thousands of samples daily, saw the administrative department staff stepping up to offer support. They created a meticulous schedule to manage personnel and recruited part-time workers to cope with the demand. However, the high demand for clinical pathologists made it challenging to find external hires, necessitating reliance on internal staff. Administrative employees were organized into several groups, each rotating to ensure continuous support.

After completing their day jobs at 5:30 p.m., supporting employees quickly grabbed dinner before heading to the testing lab. Although not qualified to conduct the specialized testing tasks, they could assist with simpler tasks like labeling specimens and verifying records. Their primary role involved sorting specimens received later in the day and ensuring their accurate registration. Often, their work stretched past midnight.

"We literally worked until we saw stars in the sky. It was hard to keep track of the days; the week just blurred together." Despite the strenuous conditions, these employees unanimously agreed that their colleagues in the testing department faced even greater challenges. They worked longer hours under more intense conditions. Rather than focusing on their own hardships, these supportive staff members chose to acknowledge and praise the extraordinary efforts of their colleagues.

There is a proverb, "Ants take and transport the mortar," which might make one wonder how such small creatures could move something so substantial. Yet, when thousands, even tens of thousands, of ants unite, they can transport loads much larger than themselves, as we've often seen with swarms of ants carrying large insects. During the COVID-19 pandemic, the relentless 365-day work schedule without weekends or holidays was daunting, but SCL employees persevered by leaning on each other. Their collective spirit and mutual support were pivotal in navigating through the immense challenges posed by the pandemic. In this way, SCL managed to withstand the overwhelming tsunami of COVID-19, buoyed by a workforce committed to supporting one another through every hardship.

PREPAREDNESS TO RESPOND TO INFECTIOUS DISEASES

On February 23, 2023, the OECD released a health policy research report titled *Are we ready for the next crisis? Investing in health system resilience.* This report placed member countries into four categories, A to D, based on the cumulative number of COVID-19 deaths per million people. Korea was categorized in Group A, denoting the lowest COVID-19 mortality rate among the members.

The OECD's evaluation highlighted Korea's COVID-19 strategy, known as the "3T strategy" — Testing, Tracing, and Treatment with Isolation. This approach was recognized as an exemplary model of a robust lockdown policy. The report particularly commended the rapid collaboration between public and private sectors in Korea, which established a nationwide testing system within just two weeks and efficiently isolated confirmed cases.

Other countries classified alongside Korea in Group A for their successful COVID-19 responses included Australia, Denmark, Finland, Iceland, Japan, New Zealand, and Norway. This grouping underscores the effective strategies these nations employed to manage and mitigate the pandemic's impact *(Reference: OECD "Korea and Japan are the most successful in COVID-19 response"...Why?, Korea Economic Daily, February 24, 2023)*.

As highlighted in a recent OECD report, Korea's establishment of a COVID-19 response system outpaced that of any other country. This swift action is undeniable evidence of Korea's leadership in managing health crises. The country excelled in securing and distributing quarantine supplies and implementing an integrated system for testing, isolating, and treating confirmed cases. Despite facing challenges from an unexpectedly rapid spread of the virus, Korea's prior preparedness paid dividends. Lessons learned from dealing with past outbreaks, such as the new flu and MERS, had already prompted the Korean government and medical community to formulate strategies for potential large-scale infectious diseases. Furthermore, Korea's national health insurance system, which is unique compared to those of many other countries, underpins a well-developed infrastructure for disease testing, diagnosis, and treatment. This foundation has been crucial in enabling a swift response to infectious diseases on a large scale.

Korea's prowess in genetic testing technology and systems is recognized globally. The process starts when clinicians collect samples such as blood, urine, and tissue and send them to testing agencies. These agencies conduct tests, analyze the results, and report them back to the doctors, who then inform patients and formulate treatment plans. The specialization in laboratory medicine has been instrumental in fortifying Korea's defenses against COVID-19.

Korea boasts approximately 100 medical institutions capable of conducting RT-PCR tests for COVID-19, including major players like SCL, Seoul National University Hospital, and Yonsei University Severance Hospital. These institutions are part of the "Big 5 testing institutions" known for their advanced capabilities. The Korean Society for Laboratory Medicine plays a crucial role in overseeing these facilities through regular molecular laboratory medicine certifications. Out of around 2,000 testing agencies nationwide, about

100 have earned genetic diagnostic certification.

When RT-PCR testing commenced on March 7, 2020, 47 institutions were initially designated as testing agencies. The Korea Centers for Disease Control and Prevention (now the Korea Disease Control and Prevention Agency) evaluated these centers by sending them 7 COVID-19 samples (4 positive and 3 negative) to establish their testing accuracy.

This broad-based, high-level laboratory medicine infrastructure demonstrated its effectiveness during the COVID-19 crisis, preventing a "testing crisis" despite several major pandemic waves. The Korea Centers for Disease Control and Prevention collaborated closely with private medical institutions to enhance response strategies. This included the formation of the Corona Task Force by the Korean Society for Laboratory Medicine shortly after the first confirmed case in January 2020.

Within days, the Korea Centers for Disease Control and Prevention and the Korean Society for Laboratory Medicine collaborated to develop diagnostic reagents, considering several methods, including those recommended by the World Health Organization (WHO). Each method was assessed for its pros and cons, leading to the development of a tailored testing protocol suitable for COVID-19. On January 29, the KCDC released the 'RT-PCR protocol,' a Korean-style reagent testing method, to companies, thereby standardizing the approach to

COVID-19 testing across the nation.

Each country employs slightly different RT-PCR protocols targeting various genes such as the RdRp gene, E gene, and N gene. Many countries, including the United States, standardize on the N gene. However, Korea, learning from international protocols, developed a multifaceted approach that targets multiple genes. The Korea Centers for Disease Control and Prevention (KCDC) granted emergency use approval for diagnostic reagents contingent upon successful performance evaluations of tests covering two or more gene regions. This strategic decision came as the COVID-19 threat level escalated from 'caution' to 'alert.'

The KCDC has been instrumental in maintaining the quality of diagnostic reagents and testing methods, promoting the development of additional diagnostic tools, and collaborating with the medical community on studies related to COVID-19 antibody formation and longevity. The agility of this response can be credited to lessons learned during the 2016 MERS outbreak, which established a robust framework for the emergency approval of diagnostic tools in response to new infectious diseases—a system that proved critical during the COVID-19 pandemic.

Initially, COVID-19 testing was slow and could not keep pace with the spread of the virus. Now, thanks to advances in domestic diagnostic capabilities, Korea can process over 200,000 tests per day, effectively managing the high demand.

A community that successfully overcomes a crisis deserves applause. Overcoming a crisis doesn't happen overnight; it's possible only when you strengthen your foundational systems and prepare for future crises in advance. If you fail to prepare, you will collapse helplessly when disaster strikes.

Korean testing agencies and biotech companies were able to respond effectively to the COVID pandemic and even grow afterwards because they had been attentive to and invested in large-scale infectious diseases long before the crisis hit. This contrasts sharply with many companies that faced crises due to COVID.

Leaders of organizations, whether in government or business, should regularly assess their crisis management capabilities. Especially for companies, rapid social changes can demand significant adjustments, and failing to respond to these changes may lead to upheaval. It's crucial to anticipate potential threats to survival, such as unexpected variables that the organization might face, and develop countermeasures in advance. Listening to the voices of field employees, observing market trends and public preferences, developing new products, upgrading existing ones, actively managing talent, fostering internal communication, and delegating authority responsibly are essential strategies for crisis response and organizational strengthening. Growth and crisis management are most effective when prepared for in advance, not at the moment of crisis.

Henry Wilson, the 18th Vice President of the United States, famously said, "A man who seeks diamonds must struggle through mud and swamp, because you cannot find them in polished stones. Diamonds are made." When everyone else is stuck in the mud and complaining, someone pulls a diamond out of it. Do you want to be the one covered in mud or the one who eventually finds a diamond? The choice is solely yours.

A PHONE CALL FROM FINLAND

TRUST IN LONG-TERM EFFORTS

The testing department staff member picked up the phone and tilted his head. "Finland? I'm too busy for a prank call," he thought.

At first, that's what he assumed it was. Nobody heeded the call, marking the beginning of the first overseas COVID-19 test request on the evening of March 20, 2020.

It was only after asking some detailed questions that the staff realized the call was legitimate and came from Mehiläinen Hospital in Finland. At that time, the number of COVID-19 patients in Finland was escalating rapidly. With a population of 5.5 million, there were about 2,400 confirmed cases per day. Adjusted to the population of Korea, this would equate to 24,000 confirmed cases. The death toll was around 40, which would scale to 400 if compared with Korea's population. Despite being an IT powerhouse, Finland had failed to anticipate the COVID-19 crisis, resulting in a shortage of diagnostic equipment and reagents. At that time, Finland could only conduct between 1,500 to 2,000 tests per day. Hospital staff briefly explained the situation and sought assistance.

Why did Finland choose Korea among so many countries? As mentioned earlier, Finland lacked the capacity to manage the rapidly increasing number of patients. Initially, Finland had an insufficient basic system. They placed orders with biotech companies for diagnostic equipment, but air traffic disruptions at the time prevented them from receiving the supplies. Struggling to obtain any equipment or reagents, they decided to request testing overseas. They considered several countries known for conducting extensive COVID-19 tests, including China, Korea, and Japan. Among them, China was widely recognized for low testing accuracy, and Japan had severe restrictions on designating large testing agencies capable of handling the necessary volume of tests. Consequently, Finland selected one laboratory each from Korea and Estonia for testing: SCL in Korea and Shin Lab in Estonia.

Why did they choose SCL among many testing agencies in Korea? The decision was likely due to SCL's consistent investment in enhancing the quality of its testing services. This commitment is evidenced by SCL's acquisition of CAP certification and the Excellent Laboratory Accreditation System. CAP certification is managed by the largest clinical pathology testing quality certification agency in the United States, while the Excellent Laboratory Accreditation System is overseen by the Korean Society for Laboratory Medicine. For over 20 years, SCL has consistently achieved the globally recognized CAP certification and Excellent Laboratory Accreditation, demonstrating its adherence to stringent standards. Additionally, it meets international quality management standards for medical laboratory institutions under ISO 15189 certification. These efforts to maintain high testing standards have been recognized both domestically and internationally, which influenced the decision by the hospital in Finland.

Ten days after the call from Finland, 100 samples were transported via cargo plane. Finland stipulated that the results be reported within 24 hours of receiving the samples and that some samples be returned. SCL promptly began testing, completing the process in about 4-5 hours and emailing the results within 7 hours of commencement. The samples were returned in a non-infectious state.

Unbeknownst to them at the time, this initial test served as a trial by Mehiläinen Hospital to assess SCL's competence. They compared the results from SCL with those from a lab in Estonia. SCL's tests showed a higher positive rate, which, when matched with the symptoms reported for the patients, demonstrated greater accuracy. Consequently, Mehiläinen Hospital selected SCL as their final testing partner.

Mehiläinen Hospital formally requested a contract for COVID-19 testing from SCL, revealing only then that the initial test had been a pre-contract trial and that SCL had been in competition with a laboratory in Estonia.

SCL reported to the Korean government that there was a request from Mehiläinen Hospital in Finland for COVID-19 testing. Previously, in anticipation of potential increases in international requests, the government had issued an official directive to testing agencies. This directive mandated that any overseas testing requests be reported to the government for approval, a measure to ensure domestic testing capabilities were not compromised due to handling increased overseas demands.

The government permitted the contract to proceed on humanitarian grounds, acknowledging the international commendations of our testing capabilities. At the time, SCL was equipped to manage 6,000 tests per day and had ramped up preparations to handle up to 10,000 tests per day in anticipation of a surge in confirmed cases. This expansion of capacity meant SCL could accommodate Finland's request without affecting domestic test processing.

The collaboration with Finland commenced in March and continued for about eight months. Finland would notify SCL a week in advance of sending the samples, which were then transported via private plane. Despite the significant costs associated with the private plane and testing, Finland prioritized the reliability of the testing over cost considerations.

Initially, when Finland sought testing from SCL, Mehiläinen Hospital had the capability to handle about 150 tests per day, which they later increased to 400, as reported by SCL officials. This situation highlights the proactive nature of Korean testing agencies and the robustness of their testing capabilities.

FAST PROCESSING, ACCURATE RESULTS

How do the samples from Finland sent for testing, travel to the SCL laboratory? Typically, COVID-19 samples are transported by airplane, securely packed to maintain integrity. To ensure the samples' safety, they are packaged using cold chain technology to keep them refrigerated for up to 72 hours and are triple-packaged in a virus-specific transport box to mitigate infection risks. However, the Finnish hospital sent the samples with five layers of packaging. Upon arrival in Korea, the samples are handled and transported by staff from the biologistics division, who hold an IATA DGR (Aviation Dangerous

Goods Regulations). They use a specialized vehicle equipped with refrigeration to transport the boxes to the laboratory.

Upon the arrival of the samples, the testing department staff verify that the information on the sample containers matches the pre-received list before proceeding with testing. The process involves extracting nucleic acid from the sample and then amplifying it to confirm the presence of the virus. Since the virus concentration varies, the nucleic acid is amplified sufficiently to ensure detection by the equipment. Typically, up to 90 samples can be tested simultaneously using RT-PCR equipment. The total testing time spans approximately 4–6 hours, with 1–2 hours needed for nucleic acid extraction, 2 hours for amplification, and over 1 hour to read the results. The core testing time is about 3 hours, and including result analysis, the entire process can be estimated to take up to 6 hours. If amplification is inadequate or the sample collection is flawed, a retest may be necessary, potentially doubling the time required.

The testing is conducted swiftly, and results are precise. Furthermore, Finland's trust in SCL has deepened due to the prompt electronic delivery of test results.

SCL became the first Korean company commissioned by an overseas hospital to conduct COVID-19 testing, exemplifying global trust in K-Quarantine and K-LAB. This news spread quickly, leading

Upon the arrival of the samples, the testing department staff verify that the information on the sample containers matches the pre-received list before proceeding with testing. The process involves extracting nucleic acid from the sample and then amplifying it to confirm the presence of the virus.

to inquiries from the government, various companies, and media outlets. The number of countries interested in SCL's testing services also increased. The general public, upon learning about Korea's first overseas COVID-19 test order through media reports, gained a new appreciation for the capabilities of the country's testing agencies.

This case, although specific to the testing field, holds valuable lessons for general companies. To gain customer trust, companies should focus on two key principles: speed and accuracy. Customers gravitate towards businesses they can rely on and prefer those that respond promptly and precisely to their needs. This forms the foundation of strong customer-company relationships.

Several companies are celebrated for their fast and accurate services. Amazon has consistently enhanced customer satisfaction with rapid delivery since its inception. FedEx, an American air express firm, has perfected a system that ensures timely delivery as per customers' specifications. The Ritz-Carlton, a worldwide hotel chain, offers immediate service responses to guest requests, often anticipating needs that guests themselves may not articulate. These companies have earned global acclaim by adhering to the fundamental business principles of responding swiftly and accurately to customer requests.

The formula for corporate success might seem straightforward, yet many companies drift away from the basics as they grow. Whenever customers visit, they should be greeted warmly, their needs listened to attentively, and their requests fulfilled promptly. Going the extra mile—like providing services that address even the unspoken needs of customers—adds significant value. SCL exemplifies this approach, not only by conducting tests quickly and accurately but by enhancing customer convenience through sending test results directly via email.

Listening to customer feedback from start to finish ensures they feel valued, fostering loyalty. Companies that promptly and precisely meet customer needs not only secure a loyal customer base but also see increased sales. Maintaining these fundamental principles solidifies customer trust and stabilizes the company's market position.

Chapter **5**

THE WORLD OF
DANCING STARS

In Thus Spoke Zarathustra, Nietzsche said,
"One must still have chaos in oneself to be able to give birth to a dancing star."
You must overcome countless pains and difficulties to shine brightly.
A company filled with such stars will be truly happy.

WHEN MANAGEMENT AND
THE UNION JOIN HANDS

"WE WON'T BE ABLE TO PAY TODAY."

A rather stiff look.

That's what the head of the HR department remembered the employees' faces looked like at the time. It was understandable. No one would be happy about their paychecks being delayed.

"We had temporary financial difficulties, so our paychecks were delayed once or twice. It had never happened before, so the employees were very flustered."

In 2015, SCL moved to its current office building, the fourth one in Seoul, following locations in Insa-dong, Jongno-gu, Dapsimni-dong, Dongdaemun-gu, and Dongbinggo-dong, Yongsan-gu. As the lab equipment and personnel continued to expand, the scale grew day by day, and the existing space was no longer big enough to accommodate the expansion. The management deliberated whether to build a new building at this time, but since the lab would have to move again if the lab size increased further, they decided to find a space that could accommodate future expansion rather than building a new one. They chose the Heungdeok IT Valley Building in Yongin City.

A specimen testing agency possesses supplies, medicines, and equipment whose volume is incomparable to general companies. The relocation took several months. As the space became larger, the goal was to expand facilities such as negative pressure facilities and PCR testing labs, reorganize the testing process, and equip personnel and advanced diagnostic equipment so that the automated testing capacity could handle 150,000 cases per day. At the time of the relocation, the testing department, consisting of 12 teams, occupied 3.5 floors (approximately 14,000 m2) for testing and research. This is the largest facility in Korea in terms of the size of a single building. As the facilities expanded in this way, they ended up spending much more than the budget they had prepared. A temporary cash crunch was inevitable.

What should we do? After much deliberation, the management decided to transparently disclose the entire situation to all employees. They explained to the labor union why the company was currently experiencing financial difficulties and politely asked for their understanding. The employees, upon learning of the company's situation, responded with confusion but also understanding.

Employees have fixed expenses such as basic living costs, credit card bills, and loan repayments, so a delayed paycheck can negatively impact their lives. On the other hand, they may also feel anxious, wondering if something more serious than a temporary issue is at play. Despite the management's transparent explanation, it was natural for employees unfamiliar with the details of the financial situation to have mixed feelings. However, the employees tolerated personal inconveniences and understood the company's circumstances.

The crisis passed quickly. The financial situation normalized, and everyone regained peace. The management enhanced welfare by operating seven shuttle buses to help employees commute to and from work. Now, seven years after the company relocated, only one bus is in operation due to changes in the employees' residences.

Unexpected management difficulties can occur at any time for a company. Whether long-term or temporary, as SCL experienced, if not well-managed, the company may lose great talent, which is unfortunate for its growth. The company must prepare a plan to wisely handle unexpected crises.

"If sharing the pain is unavoidable, management should lead by example. It is crucial to inform employees of the company's situation as accurately as possible. This isn't merely a notification but a request for understanding based on transparent disclosure of information.

Only then can employees make informed decisions about their next steps."

The head of the HR department emphasized that management's example, transparent information sharing, and fair compensation were key factors in helping the company overcome its crisis. He noted that once the company's financial situation improves, it is essential to provide compensation to employees who participated in sharing the burden. Measures such as salary increases or expanded welfare benefits could be considered.

When faced with management difficulties, some companies shift the burden onto employees. They may cut salaries, reduce welfare benefits, or lay off staff, while the CEO receives a salary increase or performance bonus. How can employees trust a management that prioritizes its own safety regardless of the company's fate?

When SCL faced management challenges, it respectfully sought understanding from employees based on factual information and refrained from awarding excessive financial rewards to management alone. After the crisis, SCL worked diligently to improve the working environment and establish a fair compensation system, ensuring that employees could work with peace of mind. It was thanks to this principled crisis management plan that SCL has successfully navigated several crises since its inception. As long as labor and management work together, no crisis is insurmountable.

HOW TO CREATE A FAMILY-LIKE COMPANY

'Labor' and 'Management' often have inherently incompatible positions. Employees are primarily interested in their salaries, while management focuses on performance and sales. Employees aim to earn as much as possible, whereas management seeks to maximize efficiency with minimal salary expenditures. Thus, when both sides prioritize their own interests, finding a compromise can be challenging, reflecting the typical dynamics of labor-management relations.

SCL is the first testing agency to establish a labor union. By law, labor and management must convene a labor-management council once every quarter. During these quarterly meetings, SCL management and the labor union engage in discussions about wages, incentive payments, and other significant issues.

The SCL labor union plays a crucial role in fostering unity and a sense of responsibility among employees. Even during several past crises, including the surge in testing demand caused by the COVID-19 virus, employees shared their work challenges and supported one another. Administrative staff grouped together to assist in the testing lab with sample classification, and the sales department routinely drove long distances early in the morning to ensure timely delivery of samples to the main office. Such cooperation would be impossible if employees did not perceive their colleagues' difficulties and the company's crisis as their own.

The most common phrase SCL employees use to describe their corporate culture or relationships among colleagues is "like family." However, in the context of corporate management, being described as a "family-like company" is no longer a compliment. The term "family" can imply a company where the CEO acts unilaterally. In such companies, the views of lower-level staff might be overlooked or ignored, and management may act arbitrarily. Responsibilities might be assigned without corresponding authority, managers may be chosen for their alignment with upper management rather than their expertise, and a top-down power structure often replaces rational and flexible communication.

However, the family-like company that SCL employees describe differs significantly from the traditional corporate connotation of that term. It refers to working relationships with strong bonds akin to those of a blood-related family. Observing the camaraderie, where each employee supports and cares for others, epitomizes a true family-like company. The head of the HR department commented, "I dare to boast, but I believe SCL's labor-management relations are commendable," even though he acknowledged his alignment with the company's perspective. Interestingly, many employees concur with this sentiment, a stark contrast to the prevalent individualism and intensifying labor-

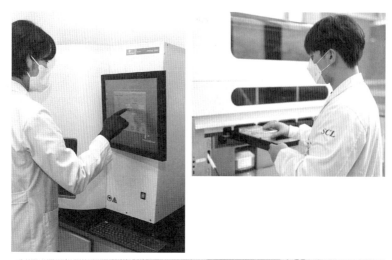

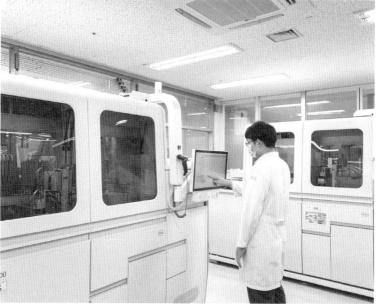

Even during several past crises, including the surge in testing demand caused by the COVID-19 virus, employees shared their work challenges and supported one another.

management conflicts elsewhere.

How is this possible? "If management prioritizes company profits and cost-cutting, it becomes challenging to work in such environments. Our management focuses more on creating an environment where employees can concentrate on their work rather than solely on sales," explained a representative.

The secret to the family-like atmosphere discussed by SCL employees lies in management's proactive approach. Although employees' demands are collected through the labor union and relayed to management, often, management acts even before these demands are formally presented. Employees inevitably trust the management, knowing that their concerns are addressed more diligently than expected.

This management attitude aligns with their pride as a medical institution committed to saving lives and as a leading global healthcare group that adheres to the principles of Evidence-Based Medicine (EBM). The management's philosophy is intricately linked to the company's operations.

The experiences of SCL employees provide valuable insights for many companies. It is widely acknowledged that 'labor' is often at a disadvantage in labor-management relations compared to 'management'. Employees struggle to voice their needs and concerns without fearing management's reaction. In contrast, management often freely expresses their desires to employees. The power dynamic is inherently skewed. Therefore, it is up to management, not the employees, to initiate engagement and bridge the gap. SCL's management has done this effectively, earning employee trust and strengthening the bonds both among employees and between labor and management.

Examining the labor-management relations of various global companies reveals that this is a critical factor affecting corporate performance. Companies that successfully forge positive labor-management relationships are likely to have a promising future, whereas those experiencing turbulent relations often face a bleak outlook in their corporate evaluations. To continue the legacy of success and maintain a leading position in the future, companies must strive for smooth labor-management agreements.

Toyota, the renowned Japanese automobile manufacturer, exemplifies maintaining cooperative labor-management relations. The company endured a period of intense conflict between a militant union and management in the 1950s. However, a shift occurred when new union executives were appointed. In 1956, these leaders introduced the Toyota Union Charter, committing to cooperative labor-management relations. By 1962, a labor-management declaration was made, stating, "the union will actively cooperate in improving productivity to stabilize employment and enhance working conditions."

Toyota's labor and management have upheld the principles of mutual trust and mutual responsibility through continued collaboration. Remarkably, Toyota management has not enacted a single layoff in over 50 years, and the union has diligently worked to boost productivity. During financial difficulties, the labor union voluntarily proposed wage restraint. Conversely, in prosperous times, management proactively suggested wage increases to the union.

In September 2020, Toyota's labor and management reached a consensus on a new wage system amidst growing market instability caused by the COVID-19 pandemic and developments in the electric vehicle market. The company proposed replacing the existing salary system, which involved uniform annual wage increases, with a job-based individual pay system focused on performance. The union initially resisted this change, expressing concerns that employees with lower performance evaluations would not receive wage increases. However, CEO Akio Toyoda personally intervened in the negotiations, leading to an agreement. This was achieved as the union recognized that enhancing competitiveness was essential to navigate the company's crisis *(Reference: Crisis Changes Corporate Culture... Will Toyota's Experiment Work?, Economic Review, October 8, 2020)*. The future implications of this change for Toyota's management remain uncertain, but such collaborative efforts between labor and management provide a hopeful prospect for overcoming crises.

Southwest Airlines exemplifies a distinctive labor-management culture compared to other airlines. The management at Southwest avoids layoffs, wage cuts, and rarely employs part-time workers or outsources contracts. Additionally, union strikes are almost nonexistent. Although there are multiple labor unions, they do not collectively pressure management. Prior to labor-management negotiations, representatives conduct surveys among employees to bridge any gaps between them and management, incorporating the findings into the negotiation process *(Reference: Hidden Power - People, Charles O'Reilly et al.,)*. Employees at Southwest describe their relationship with management as "family-like".

In its early days, Southwest Airlines faced significant challenges, including a small customer base and financial instability. However, the employees, many of whom had been laid off from other airlines, were deeply committed to the airline's success. They voluntarily cleaned cabins and organized luggage to enhance the customer experience. Impressed by the evident cooperation between labor and management, customers became repeat patrons, leading to increased sales. This concerted effort is credited with transforming Southwest into the largest low-cost airline in the United States, as reported by Gyeongbuk Daily on October 30, 2019.

However, the departure of founder Herb Kelleher marked a shift in management style, with increasing reliance on part-time workers and reductions in personnel. It remains to be seen whether these changes will alter the company's legacy and how it is perceived in the future.

Similarly, Starbucks has been a paragon of respectful labor-management relations. Howard Schultz, Starbucks' Chairman, once emphasized the importance of prioritizing employees, stating, "Employees come before customers," and "If management puts employees first, employees will put customers first." This philosophy highlights Starbucks' commitment to valuing its workforce. Efforts to foster a collegial atmosphere included using nicknames for all employees, including the CEO, and maintaining an open bulletin board for free expression of opinions. Furthermore, when customers offer praise, the commended employees are celebrated by their peers, boosting morale and work motivation.

Recently, Starbucks is seeing significant changes. For the first time since its establishment, a union has been formed within the company, spurred by employee reductions during the COVID-19 pandemic and a subsequent increase in workload. The company is now facing a lawsuit from the National Labor Relations Board (NLRB) for allegedly threatening to withhold welfare benefits and wage increases from union members. This shift from harmony to conflict raises questions about whether labor and management can still deliver satisfactory services to customers. Investors are closely monitoring the potential negative impacts of this labor-management conflict on corporate performance.

Historically, labor-management relations, with their fundamentally opposing positions, are rarely completely amicable. Many globally recognized companies that previously achieved remarkable results through strong labor-management relations are now facing internal strife marked by severe conflict. While conflict is a natural part of human interaction, when it escalates to the point of deep mutual harm, it hinders progress towards common goals. If labor and management pull in opposite directions, they risk losing their way and drifting aimlessly rather than moving towards their objectives. It is crucial for both parties to consider how such conflicts may affect their company's image in the eyes of customers and investors.

While expressing pride in SCL's labor-management relations, the head of the HR department cautioned, "No matter how strong our current relationship is, it'll not always be smooth sailing. Sometimes, we will face storms." This is a realistic perspective; even the best relationships can be tested during crises. Therefore, it's crucial for both labor and management to establish guiding principles for their relationship. This approach mirrors Toyota's strategy of adhering to previously set principles of mutual trust and mutual responsibility, even in times of crisis. With solid principles in place, the organization can withstand turbulence without faltering.

The first principle for maintaining smooth labor-management relations is mutual understanding and consideration of each other's positions, recognizing that differences of opinion will exist. 'Labor' should be considerate towards 'management's' needs, while 'management' must ensure job security and fair compensation for employees. Ultimately, labor-management relations are viable only as long as the company itself exists. If ongoing conflicts threaten the company's survival, it becomes a lose-lose situation for both sides.

The second principle involves creating a forum for open dialogue between labor and management. SCL adheres to this by conducting quarterly consultations with the labor union, as mandated by law. Regular, structured dialogue helps bridge differing viewpoints. Additionally, establishing a channel for employees to express their thoughts freely can enhance engagement. In many workplaces, hierarchical structures and busy schedules can deter employees from voicing their opinions. Creating a platform, similar to the open bulletin board that Starbucks implemented, where employees can openly share their thoughts—and having those opinions acknowledged—encourages active participation and contributes to a healthier workplace environment.

Throughout its 40-year history, SCL has faced numerous crises, overcoming each not through the singular efforts of a standout individual, but through the collective dedication and hard work of its employees. This history makes it clear that excellent labor-management relations are crucial for corporate growth. As Aesop famously said, "United we stand, divided we fall."

A COMPANY EVERYONE WANTS TO WORK FOR

REASONS FOR HAVING MANY LONG-TERM EMPLOYEES

What kind of company do you want to work for? This is likely the most pressing question for job seekers. Naturally, they seek a good company—one that ensures fair compensation for the work performed, offers a robust welfare system, and possesses a clear vision for the future. These are the hallmarks of what people consider a good company.

Then, how do you determine if a company is good or not? The best way to gauge a company's quality is by exploring its reputation. In today's digital age, the reach of social media means that opinions can circulate globally without a sound. If you're curious, you can easily discover how a company treats its employees. However, with the prevalence of misinformation, it's advisable to seek insights directly from current employees. While companies can cultivate favorable public images, they cannot disguise reality from their employees, who experience the company's operations firsthand. Thus, truly good companies are not those with merely a stellar external reputation, but those that are genuinely praised by their employees, who enjoy their work environment and feel valued.

When discussing customer satisfaction management, employees are essentially considered to be internal customers. This perspective shifts the view of employees from mere labor providers to 'customers who must be satisfied first.' As internal customers, employees not only produce the company's products or services but are also the first to use and evaluate them. Their experience can greatly influence their testimonials; if they are satisfied, they will share positive stories, and if dissatisfied, they might spread negative feedback. Therefore, prioritizing the satisfaction of internal customers—employees—before external customers is a crucial strategy that significantly impacts a company's performance. This approach explains why companies highly praised by their employees are often recognized as outstanding businesses.

SCL has retained many long-term employees over its 40-year history, with most maintaining a lasting relationship with the company despite a few ups and downs.

In customer satisfaction management, employees are regarded as internal customers. This perspective encourages companies to see employees not merely as labor providers but as "customers who must be satisfied first."

SCL also earned a favorable reputation. Employees readily describe SCL as a true family-like company and often refer it to their college friends. This word-of-mouth endorsement is so strong that it's common during job interviews to encounter applicants who say, "I applied because a senior from my school recommended this company." It's rare to find young employees at SCL who resign just a few months after struggling to get hired, if they find the company unsuitable.

Chairman Lee Kyoung Ryul attributes SCL's employee loyalty to "servitude and consideration." This golden rule—treat others as you would like to be treated—is central to all of SCL's treatment and welfare policies. The management's attitude of servitude and consideration motivates employees to excel in their roles. High performance is recognized and credited by the management, creating a pleasant working environment and a virtuous cycle of mutual growth.

MOTHER'S CANCER DISCOVERED THROUGH FAMILY CHECKUP

How does SCL serve its employees? The company ensures job security, appropriate compensation, and performance-based incentives. Additionally, it offers a variety of welfare benefits regarded as benchmarks in the industry, including support for in-house clubs and children's tuition.

In-house clubs, for instance, play a significant role in revitalizing employees overwhelmed by their workload. SCL is proud of its many clubs across the nation, including at its headquarters and 62 customer centers. Notable among these is 'Arumduri,' a gardening club mainly comprised of female employees from the testing and administrative departments. It serves as a healing community where members exchange plant care tips and share flowers monthly, fostering a supportive and nurturing environment.

"I feel comforted when I see colorful flowers after wrestling with specimens all day. On days when there is a club meeting, I go to work with anticipation."

The company's in-house baseball club, founded in 2011 by employees from the sales, testing, and administrative departments, has been an active participant in the social baseball league ever since. Achieving 4th place in the 2013 regular season and second place in the playoffs, and winning the regular season in 2018 with another second-place finish in the playoffs, the club has significantly fostered interdepartmental understanding and camaraderie, greatly enhancing communication and overall work life.

Given the high number of female employees, SCL has established a robust welfare system focused on pregnancy, childbirth, and childcare. The company hires temporary substitutes for employees on maternity or childcare leave, a practice not universally adopted in all companies. Often, employees in other organizations feel uneasy taking maternity or childcare leave due to the lack of interim replacements, leading to increased workload for remaining staff. However, at SCL, this proactive approach ensures that those on leave can rest without worry, and their colleagues are not burdened with extra work. This policy has resulted in a high rate of employees returning to work post-leave without facing any discrimination. Furthermore, SCL actively supports the operation of workplace-type daycare centers, promoting a work-life balance and contributing to efforts to address the low birth rate challenge.

The welfare system at SCL, a healthcare group, is uniquely suited to its business characteristics. It supports annual health checkups and flu vaccinations not only for employees but also for their families, covering up to six family members. This service is facilitated through the Hanaro Medical Foundation, part of the same group, ensuring comprehensive healthcare support.

One employee, referred to here as Employee A, shared a particularly poignant experience. During a routine colonoscopy provided by the company, a polyp was discovered. Initially, it didn't seem serious, but the biopsy revealed early-stage rectal cancer. Fortunately, thanks to the early detection, she underwent a resection and made a full recovery. Without the checkup, the cancer might have been detected too late. She credits her survival to the company-provided health checkup.

Another employee, Employee B, discovered his mother's liver cancer through a company-supported family checkup.

"She never complained of feeling sick, and we often overlook the liver because it's a silent organ."

The cancer was caught just before it could metastasize, and his mother underwent successful surgery and chemotherapy. B expressed deep gratitude for the welfare benefits that allowed for early detection, shuddering at the thought of what might have been if the diagnosis had come later.

SCL's diverse welfare systems are part of its strategy to create a 'good workplace to work in.' By providing a supportive and caring environment, SCL not only motivates its employees to work diligently but also attracts talent and reduces turnover rates. Employees who are satisfied with their workplace and see a clear vision for the future see no reason to seek employment elsewhere. Their attachment to the company and passion for their work lead to improved performance. In essence, enhancing the work environment and offering comprehensive welfare benefits are strategic moves that boost both productivity and profitability for the company.

WELFARE SYSTEM THAT BOOSTS WORK MORALE
AND PROMOTES COMPANY GROWTH

Global companies are implementing various welfare systems to enhance their employees' quality of life and increase focus at work. Airbnb, a leading global accommodation brokerage firm, has adopted a flexible work model that allows employees to work from anywhere, domestically or internationally, for up to 90 days per year. This policy was implemented with the understanding that remote work capabilities would attract top talent, including those living far from company offices. Despite the geographical dispersion, Airbnb maintains cohesion and teamwork through regular departmental meetings and social events, ensuring that the collaborative spirit is not lost.

In June 2022, Airbnb introduced a unified wage system across countries, adjusting salaries in lower-wage regions to match those in higher-wage areas. CEO Brian Chesky has stated that this flexibility in work location and schedule fosters creativity and innovation, ultimately boosting work motivation *(Reference: "Introduction of a work system that allows employees to work freely anywhere," Airbnb News, April 28, 2022).*

Patagonia, a U.S.-based eco-friendly outdoor brand, is known for its remarkably low employee turnover rate, which stands at about 4%, significantly below the average 60% turnover in the U.S. retail sector. This low rate indicates high employee satisfaction within the company. What makes Patagonia such a desirable place to work?

Patagonia operates under a flexible work hour system aptly named "Let My People Go Surfing." This policy allows employees to work when they are most productive and rest when needed, encouraging them to surf when the waves are good and ski following fresh snowfalls.

In its hiring process, Patagonia applies criteria different from those typically valued by other companies. They seek employees who are passionate about environmental protection and who demonstrate independent and creative thinking. When an employee considers leaving, CEO Yvon Chouinard personally conducts exit interviews to understand what the company may be lacking. This sincere and earnest approach impresses employees, highlighting Chouinard's commitment to continuous improvement.

Patagonia has also established an in-house kindergarten early in its history, allowing employees to focus on their work knowing their children are nearby, enjoying their day under the care of excellent teachers. At day's end, parents and children leave together, reinforcing the balance between work and family life. Chouinard emphasizes that work should be enjoyable, famously stating, "Work should be fun. It should be so exciting to come to work that employees have to jump up the stairs two at a time" *(Reference: Patagonia, Surfing When the Waves Hit, Yvon Chouinard).* His philosophy ensures that the workplace is both fun and comfortable.

Salesforce is an American IT company specializing in cloud computing services for businesses. Although it is not widely recognized by the general public, Salesforce has a robust global presence, serving many international companies. It expanded into Korea a few years ago, where it now provides services to numerous large companies, establishing a significant market presence.

In 2018, Salesforce was named the best company to work for by *Fortune* an American business magazine. The company's corporate culture is encapsulated by the Hawaiian word "Ohana," which means "family." Salesforce CEO Marc Benioff champions a strong sense of family and responsibility among all employees. Despite their busy schedules, employees generally do not feel overwhelmed by their workload. Management not only monitors goal achievement through a work management system but also ensures that employees' quality of life is maintained. Amenities such as free breakfast, snacks, and drinks are provided, along with subsidized transportation expenses. Furthermore, Salesforce offers unlimited paid vacation, allowing employees to take as much time off as they need, and a wellness program to promote health.

Microsoft also offers unlimited paid vacation, though this benefit is restricted to full-time employees. Additionally, there is a separate provision for a 10-day vacation specifically for sickness or rest. Microsoft's campus includes various in-house sports and entertainment facilities, and for added convenience, there is a beauty salon and hospital on-site *(Reference: "Rest as much as you want"... MS introduces 'unlimited vacation system', Chosun Biz, January 12, 2023).*

Recently, many companies in Silicon Valley, including Google, have announced plans to scale back their in-house welfare systems and reduce their workforce significantly. Among the companies previously mentioned, Salesforce has eliminated its "Wellness Day", which allowed employees to take a day off once a month to promote health. This decision is a response to rapidly changing market conditions, declining performance, and economic downturn.

When the business environment deteriorates, companies often have no choice but to reduce welfare benefits. Although these temporary changes are inevitable, many companies recognize the positive impact of welfare systems. Welfare systems are an effective means of boosting employee motivation and improving corporate productivity. Examining welfare initiatives from exemplary companies, including SCL, shows that health promotion programs, childcare leave systems, and performance-based incentives are popular among employees. Companies need to develop welfare systems that reflect employees' preferences while maintaining a consistent level in the ever-changing business environment. If many benefits are introduced during times of high sales and then removed when sales decline, it can undermine trust between labor and management. Therefore, it is advisable for companies to be consistent in their commitments to employees. By creating and consistently maintaining a welfare system suited to their unique situations, companies can foster solidarity between labor and management, enhance work motivation, improve performance, and become places where excellent talent chooses to stay for the long term.

HUMAN, ALL TOO HUMAN

EACH AND EVERY PERSON IS IMPORTANT

In Antoine de Saint-Exupéry's *The Little Prince*, there's a poignant conversation between the Little Prince and the fox: "The most difficult thing in the world is for a person to win another person's heart... It is really difficult to make that windy heart stay."

Few would disagree with this sentiment. As the proverb goes, "You can know ten feet of water, but not one foot of a person's heart." A person's heart is elusive and hard to win.

However, SCL has successfully won the hearts of its employees. This achievement likely stems from its emphasis on servitude and consideration as core elements of its corporate culture, supplemented by various welfare systems. Employees point out another crucial factor: the way the company views people.

"There is a strong tendency to maintain relationships once they're formed, something like a warm gaze looking at people. It may be hard for others to understand, but that is how we feel."

Mistakes happen in the workplace, and sometimes their consequences are more significant than anticipated. Since a company is fundamentally an interest group, it is challenging to tolerate actions detrimental to management. Employees who err are typically disciplined, and in severe cases, dismissed. However, SCL takes a different approach by giving employees a chance to rectify their mistakes rather than immediately reprimanding them.

The same philosophy applies to performance. Generally, companies set individual goals and push employees to meet them, creating an atmosphere of pressure and stress. This is true across all departments, not just sales. However, SCL employees report a different experience.

"All departments, including testing and sales, have performance indicators and targets, but rather than feeling pressured by these goals, the company understands that if we do our jobs well, good results will naturally follow. That's why the company works hard to support each department member and create an environment conducive to achieving good results."

SCL sets and manages goals, but it prioritizes enabling each team member to maximize their capabilities within their roles over merely

The most important value in all aspects of management at SCL, including organizational operations, personnel management, and strategy formulation, is people.

pressuring them to achieve these targets. For instance, in the testing department, even when the number of tests increases, the focus remains on minimizing errors and optimizing work processes, rather than just meeting deadlines. If it becomes clear that the workload consistently surpasses employee capabilities, management explores alternatives such as augmenting staff or upgrading equipment.

While most companies strive to maximize efficiency with minimal capital, SCL operates differently, valuing people over performance. When employees observe management proactively creating improvement plans, they feel motivated to commit long-term to the company, reinforcing their trust in the organization.

As Chairman Lee Kyoung Ryul explains, "The most significant characteristic of the healthcare field in which we work is its emphasis on people. People are the ones who save lives; they are both the beginning and the culmination of our efforts, which inherently makes them crucial. This focus could be perceived as a vulnerability, but it can also be a strength."

At SCL, diverse professionals including doctors, clinical pathologists, and researchers with advanced degrees collaborate on research, experiments, and tests—all aimed at enhancing human health. While each expert has a distinct role, producing results involves collective input and deliberation. Regardless of the level of automation, it is essential for people to analyze and interpret what the machines process, emphasizing the importance of human collaboration. Drawing inspiration from Friedrich Nietzsche's philosophy, SCL's corporate culture, described as "all too human," is intentionally designed around these principles.

PRODUCTIVITY IMPROVEMENT & EMPLOYEE SATISFACTION TRAINING AIMED AT CATCHING TWO BIRDS WITH ONE STONE

At SCL, a professional is defined not just by their deep knowledge and experience in a particular field, but also by their ability to collaborate effectively with others. This collaborative spirit among SCL professionals is fostered by a strong sense of pride in their work and support from the company through training in communication, cooperation, and professional mission. To this end, SCL has established the SCL Academy, an innovative platform dedicated to nurturing employee skills and understanding of their roles and callings.

Launched in March 2020, the SCL Academy was the first of its kind among testing agencies to provide an online education center specifically for its employees. The shift from traditional face-to-face education to online learning was accelerated by the COVID-19 pandemic, focusing on enhancing two-way communication and empathy through digital means. The Academy facilitates rapid and engaging training for employees across various locations, including SCL headquarters, Daegu Hospital, Jeju Hospital, and nationwide branch offices.

The first director of the Academy was Professor Emeritus Lee Kyung-won, formerly of Yonsei University College of Medicine. The Academy also features lectures from esteemed professors from top domestic universities and SCL specialists, ensuring high-quality programming.

The online education center at the Academy offers comprehensive training and education in legal matters, general knowledge, specific class instructions, and job-specific skills. Moving forward, SCL plans to focus on practical and fieldwork-oriented education, beginning with online courses. The Academy not only produces its own educational content but also integrates materials through partnerships with leading content production companies. By collecting training requests from employees via surveys, the Academy is able to provide tailored educational content across various fields, significantly enhancing both productivity and employee satisfaction.

Many companies invest time and money in training their employees because developing their work skills and knowledge through training can enhance productivity and profitability. In a world that changes rapidly and where new technologies emerge every minute, mastering these can also pave the way for developing innovative future products. Employees feel empowered as they enhance their abilities through training, and their job satisfaction increases because they can receive appropriate compensation and incentives when the company's sales rise.

LIKE AN AFRICAN ELEPHANT LEADING ITS HERD

African elephants are the largest land animals and are renowned for their excellent social skills. Typically, an older female elephant becomes the leader of the herd, guiding elephants of the same bloodline. These elephants protect each other from predators such as lions and tigers, and they collaboratively work to safeguard their calves from becoming prey. Mother elephants teach their offspring essential survival skills.

When searching for food, the lead elephant communicates the route and water sources to the herd. They cooperate to overcome obstacles, and if any member falls into a ditch or mud, they unite to assist in the rescue. When they encounter an elderly elephant or one wounded by predators, they stay with it for a considerable time, demonstrating loyalty by visiting the site before moving on to a new area. Although humans pride themselves on possessing the highest intelligence and emotional capabilities on Earth, the behaviors exhibited by African elephants are truly astonishing *(Reference: African elephant, Wikipedia)*. When discussing the talent profile of SCL, a company that deeply values people, one is reminded of African elephants. SCL seeks individuals who not only excel in their roles but also possess a strong sense of cooperation. While innovation is crucial in the life sciences field where SCL operates, the company places a higher value on sincerity, daily diligence, and the ability to collaborate effectively. In terms of leadership, SCL prefers those who can lead through logic and persuasion rather than through charisma alone. Such leaders are not focused solely on personal credit but are committed to the success of their team members.

Chairman Lee Kyoung Ryul has emphasized that respect for individuals should underpin every interaction, regardless of one's position. He asserts that respect as a leader must be earned through actions, not demanded through authority:

"Raising your voice and reprimanding others does not effectively motivate team members. A true leader inspires their team to excel independently, without resorting to coercive methods."

Given SCL's emphasis on collaboration, the company values the collective power of ordinary people over the brilliance of a solitary genius. With many tasks requiring teamwork, it is beneficial for individuals to excel, but more importantly, the company needs people who can listen to others' opinions and work collaboratively to produce results.

SCL operates by delegating authority and responsibility to each department head, rather than centralizing power within its top management, including the chairman. This approach allows each team the autonomy to operate according to its unique characteristics and the individuality of its members. As a result, SCL's corporate culture exhibits a diverse array of styles across different departments. Department heads lead by setting goals, coaching their team members, and advancing together.

The traits that SCL values align with those sought by many other companies. According to a 2022 survey by the job search platform Saramin, which involved 538 companies, the most valued "talent keywords" were responsibility (52.7%, multiple responses), followed by communication skills (32.9%), sincerity (32.9%), teamwork (28.6%), positive attitude (25.1%), and professionalism (16.5%). Additionally, 77% of companies reported eliminating candidates with impressive resumes that did not match their ideal profile, while 86.1% hired candidates with less-than-perfect resumes who were a better fit *(Reference: "Specifications? Now it's a battle for ideal candidates! This is the People Companies Want to Hire," Case News, March 11, 2022).*

This shift toward valuing personality and qualifications over mere talent and ability is a recent trend. A 2021 survey by Job Korea of 578 domestic companies about hiring criteria during an economic downturn found that positivity was most valued (48.8%), followed by sincerity (46.3%), perseverance (44.9%), responsibility (30.3%), and proactiveness (22.3%) *(Reference: "Korean companies are drastically revising their ideal candidates for 2021!", Job Korea, March 27, 2021).*

In a 2020 Saramin survey involving 334 companies, responsibility (17.4%) again ranked first, trailed by sincerity (15.9%), professionalism (12.3%), and cooperation/teamwork (11.1%). The survey noted that a candidate's fit with the company's talent profile influenced hiring decisions 58.1% of the time, with 82.6% of companies having hired candidates with less-than-perfect resumes because they fit the talent profile, and 79.3% having rejected candidates with strong resumes who did not fit *(Reference: "The No. 1 corporate talent profile is responsibility," News Tomato, February 10, 2020).*

Many job seekers focus on crafting impressive resumes, but companies are increasingly valuing preferred talents over mere qualifications. This shift recognizes that an individual's personality and fundamental qualities often outweigh outstanding abilities for organizational success. HR managers note that the talents driving company growth are not isolated geniuses but those who can humbly collaborate as part of a team. SCL actively recruits and nurtures such talents. Each member is respected for their unique contributions and works alongside colleagues to achieve a shared vision.

In today's world, the emphasis has moved away from singular genius. To stand out in an organization, one should prioritize personality and inherent qualities. Remember, the ability to complete tasks faithfully and responsibly and to communicate effectively with team members is now considered the most crucial virtue in a candidate.

CORPORATE PHILOSOPHY SUSTAINED FOR 40 YEARS

WALKING GOOD STEPS FOR SIX MINUTES

347,182 people. 1,165 types.

What do these numbers represent? The first is the number of rare disease patients registered with the Korea Disease Control and Prevention Agency (KDCA 2020 Rare Disease Patient Statistical Yearbook), and the second represents the number of rare diseases identified (KDCA announcement, December 23, 2022). A rare disease is defined as one that affects fewer than 20,000 people or whose prevalence is difficult to ascertain due to diagnostic challenges. Each year, the KDCA designates certain rare diseases for national management under the "Rare Disease Management Act."

Medical experts indicate that the official records underrepresent the actual number of rare diseases affecting patients. Globally, there are over 7,000 known rare diseases, and many people suffer without realizing they have one.

Patients with rare diseases face significant hardships due to a lack of specialists and available treatments or medications. Obtaining a diagnosis can be so challenging that patients frequently move from one hospital to another in search of answers. Many medications are not covered by insurance, making treatment costs a substantial burden. For diseases not listed under the "Rare Disease Management Act," medical support is unavailable, and even if a disease is designated as rare, out-of-pocket expenses such as non-covered costs, selective coverage, reserve coverage, and fees for double or triple room hospitalization remain the patient's responsibility. Being ill is difficult enough, but the additional financial strain and lack of understanding can lead to a severe emotional crisis.

To address these challenges, there is a campaign called "Walking Good Steps for Six Minutes." Inspired by the six-minute walk test, which assesses the walking ability of patients with rare and chronic diseases, this campaign aims to raise social awareness about rare diseases. Participants walk for six minutes on a path made of gravel or acupressure plates to empathize with the struggles of these patients. The steps taken are converted into monetary donations.

SCL participated in the "Walking Good Steps for Six Minutes" campaign held in Gwanghwamun on May 23 to commemorate

Rare Disease Overcoming Day that was designated in 2017. Over 3,000 citizens, 58 volunteers, and six organizations, including the Seoul Metropolitan Government, Korea Volunteer Culture, Sanofi Genzyme, the Korean Society of Medical Genetics, the Life Insurance Social Contribution Foundation, and SCL, joined the event to empathize with patients and support their recovery. SCL employees expressed a profound sense of accomplishment from their participation.

"Since I work at a testing agency, I am knowledgeable about rare diseases. However, participating in the event deepened my sense of mission as I experienced firsthand the challenges faced by these patients."

Early diagnosis is crucial for managing rare diseases, highlighting the pivotal role of testing agencies. The event reinforced the employees' commitment to their responsibilities as healthcare workers.

ENSURING NO ONE SUFFERS ALONE

SCL is dedicated to fulfilling its social responsibilities as a medical institution and global healthcare company, particularly focusing on supporting underprivileged groups in the community. The company has signed an MOU with local organizations, including Suwon City, for the "Health Sharing Happiness Companionship, Support Project for the Vulnerable." This initiative funds various projects, including providing air conditioners for bed-bound patients and utility bill assistance for the economically disadvantaged.

In collaboration with the Gyeonggi-do branch of the Korean Red Cross, SCL launched the 'Sister's Gift' project to provide sanitary products to underprivileged female youth in the region. This initiative addresses the difficulties these young women face in affording basic necessities like sanitary pads. Additionally, SCL has partnered with the Gyeonggi Province branch of the Korean Red Cross to support medical staff fighting COVID-19 by providing relief supplies. The company also donated COVID-19 self-diagnosis kits to the Seongnam City and Anyang City Youth Foundations and supported quarantine efforts, including COVID-19 testing for athletes and officials at the '2022 Incheon SK Telecom Grand Prix.' In response to heavy rain damage in 2022, SCL assisted flood victims and donated computers to 32 local children's centers in Yongin City.

Recently, SCL has initiated a project to provide IT education to underprivileged children. In cooperation with local children's centers, the company identifies children in need and offers an education program that covers essential IT knowledge, from basic computer skills to coding. Members of the SCL Information Systems Department have volunteered as instructors for this program, with plans to expand the IT education initiative in the future.

SCL's enduring social contribution activities also include the 'Rising Again Clinic' and the 'Love Sharing Blood Drive.' The Rising Again Clinic offers free testing services to homeless individuals with compromised health and has been operational since 2009. To date, 4,677 homeless individuals have received free tests in 72 categories, including electrolytes and tumor markers. The Love Sharing Blood Drive, a collaboration with Chung-Ang University Hospital since 2013, aims to alleviate the national blood shortage and foster a culture of sharing within the community.

In 2022, SCL signed an agreement with Korea Employment Agency for Perons with Disabilities (kead) to establish a subsidiary-type standard workplace to create jobs for disabled individuals. In partnership with its affiliate, Hanaro Medical Foundation, SCL jointly opened a café named 'Hove' in Cheongjin-dong, Jongno-gu, Seoul, where ten disabled baristas are employed. SCL Healthcare plans to expand this café business into the Yongin area, including Gangnam.

Beyond collaborative social contribution activities, Chairman Lee Kyoung Ryul and SCL employees also engage in independent initiatives. A prime example is the 'Hope Sharing Challenge', a participatory social contribution activity where donations for children with disabilities are raised in proportion to the health challenges completed by SCL employees.

As a medical institution and global healthcare company, SCL is deeply committed to fulfilling its social responsibilities through diverse and impactful social contribution activities.

SCL is also committed to international social contribution, particularly in supporting third countries. Through the Gipum Nanum (Joy Sharing Foundation) an international relief and development NPO specializing in education, SCL sponsored a vehicle to the Cambodian disabled technical school 'Banteay Prieb'. Located in Phnom Penh, Banteay Prieb is a technical school that identifies disabled students overlooked by welfare services and supports their independence through technical education and employment opportunities.

In 2022, in collaboration with Yonsei University College of Medicine Yongin Severance Hospital and Yongin Immigrant Support Center, SCL supported treatment costs for Mongolian patients struggling with incurable diseases. This initiative enabled a 15-year-old Mongolian boy suffering from heart failure, whose symptoms had not improved with previous treatments, to come to Korea for a precise diagnosis and appropriate treatment.

In 2023, to celebrate its 40th anniversary, SCL participated in a volunteer activity at the bakery sharing center, organized in cooperation with the Central Volunteer Center of the Gyeonggi Province Branch of the Korean Red Cross. Employees and their children made and packaged 400 loaves of bread with great care, which were then distributed to vulnerable families and facilities in Yongin and Seongnam.

SCL's consistent engagement in social contribution activities stems from its commitment to not leaving anyone to suffer alone. This commitment aligns with SCL's 'people-centered' corporate philosophy, which has been fundamental since its inception 40 years ago. As a medical institution and a global healthcare group, SCL sees it as its natural duty to alleviate the hardships of those suffering from illness and those in welfare blind spots.

Therefore, SCL's social contribution activities extend beyond financial support; they deeply engage with the local community to address real issues. The company actively leverages its extensive network of medical staff and experts for social causes, providing varied support where it is most needed, such as medical assistance, quarantine supplies, and daily necessities.

SCL's diverse and active approach to social contribution has garnered significant recognition. At the 2023 Chosun Ilbo Social Contribution Awards Ceremony, SCL was honored with the grand prize in the job creation category. Beyond these activities, SCL has also been widely acknowledged for its efforts in promoting the mutual prosperity of local communities. This is reflected in its hiring practices post-COVID-19; as of 2022, employee recruitment increased by more than 50% compared to 2019. Moreover, the proportion of disabled employees at SCL, which has been rising continuously since 2016, now stands at approximately 3% of the total workforce.

SCL'S MAJOR SOCIAL CONTRIBUTION ACTIVITIES (2021-2023)

- SCL Social Welfare Association, support for multicultural families in preparation for Chuseok (2021)

  [Jointly with Korea Institute For Healthy Family of Jiguchon Welfare Foundation]

  - Delivery of meal kits in preparation for Chuseok to 200 alien workers and international students living in Yongin City who have difficulty visiting their home countries during the Chuseok holidays due to COVID-19

- Support for cervical cancer vaccination for women in medically vulnerable groups (2022)

  [Jointly with the Gyeonggi Health Support Center of Dongnam Health University]

  - Support for cervical cancer vaccination for women at the Elim Protection Workshop, a welfare facility for the disabled, and Suwon City Cultural Center

- Donation to Uijeongbu City's '100-day Love Relay' (2022)

  [Support for participation in the Uijeongbu Citizens' Love Sharing Campaign, which participates in a 100-day relay-style donation]

  - Support for residents in need of a helping hand, such as families in crisis and vulnerable groups who are experiencing economic difficulties due to COVID-19 Support

• Support for Yongin City's 'Love Sharing Kimchi Festival' (2022)

[Jointly with Yongin City Volunteer Center]

- Participation in the 'Love Sharing Kimchi Festival' for vulnerable residents with Yongin City Volunteer Center
- Support for kimchi material costs for 500 vulnerable households and participation of employee volunteers

• Donation of ponchos to model drivers in Yongin City with ponchos (2022)

[Jointly with Yongin City Volunteer Center]

- Donation of ponchos for traffic control volunteers in congested areas

• Donation of 10,000 COVID-19 diagnostic kits to Jeju Regional Children's Centers (2022)

[Jointly with Jeju Community Chest Of Korea and Jeju Special Self-Governing Province Regional Children's Center Association]

- Donation of COVID-19 self-diagnosis kits to 65 regional children's centers in Jeju

• Support for social contribution projects to promote health of socially vulnerable groups in Jeju (2022)

[Jointly with Jeju Community Chest Of Korea and Link]

- Support medical expenses for vulnerable groups in Jeju Island who cannot afford treatment costs

- Seocho-gu Yeouicheon Walking Trail Maintenance Environmental Campaign (2022)

  [Jointly with Seocho-gu and Seocho-gu Volunteer Center]
  - 'Yeouicheon Trail Maintenance' environmental campaign as part of carbon neutrality practices
  - Sponsorship of 3,000 seedlings along the Yeouicheon Trail

- Donation of 'Santa's Gift' to local children's centers (2022)
  - Donation of Santa's Gift (school supplies set) to children at local children's centers with donations raised through employee walk donations in the 'Hope Sharing Challenge'

- Emergency relief supplies for Türkiye evacuees (2023)
  - Donation of relief supplies such as winter clothing, quilts, and blankets voluntarily donated by employees to Türkiye earthquake victims

- Listed on the 'Red Cross Honors Company RCHC' (2023)
  - Donation of W100 million to the Gyeonggi Province branch of the Korean Red Cross
  - Various support projects for the vulnerable, such as packaging and delivering side dishes and baking volunteer work
  - Listed on RCHC, a large-scale donation program of the Gyeonggi Province branch of the Korean Red Cross

- Participation in the 'Company with Good Spending' campaign of the Korean Red Cross (2023)
  - Participation in the company's regular sponsorship program to support families in economic crisis
  - Donation of funds needed for customized welfare projects for vulnerable families, such as livelihood, medical, and housing support

- Bread-making volunteer work for employees and their children in commemoration of the 40th anniversary of the foundation (2023)
  - Bread-making and packaging at the Central Volunteer Center of the Gyeonggi-do branch of the Korean Red Cross
  - Participation of SCL employees and their children
  - Donation of 400 items to vulnerable families and related facilities in Yongin and Seongnam

Red Cross Honors Corporate Membership Ceremony. The reason SCL has consistently engaged in social contribution activities is that it does not want to leave anyone to suffer alone. This is in line with SCL's 'people-centered' corporate philosophy, which has been upheld for 40 years since its establishment.

COMPANIES FULFILLING THEIR SOCIAL RESPONSIBILITIES

Companies fulfilling their social responsibilities undertake activities in which a company voluntarily meets the social obligations expected and demanded by its stakeholders—workers, consumers, local communities, civic groups, governments, etc. CSR is typically divided into four stages. The first stage is 'economic responsibility,' which involves maximizing profits and creating jobs. The second stage is 'legal responsibility,' encompassing accounting transparency, honest tax payments, and the protection of consumer rights. The third stage is 'ethical responsibility,' which addresses responsibilities towards the environment, ethical management, product safety, and the fair treatment of women, locals, and minorities. The fourth stage is 'philanthropic responsibility,' referring to the company's support for social contribution activities or charities, and contributions to education, culture, and sports activities *(Reference: Corporate Social Responsibility, Dictionary of Current Economic Terms, Ministry of Strategy and Finance)*. The activities of SCL fall under this fourth stage.

CSR is fundamentally an ethical or moral obligation without legal enforceability. However, an increasing number of companies are incorporating CSR into their corporate strategies to enhance their internal and external images and ultimately increase profits. From the company's perspective, CSR is a means to boost profits, while consumers, local communities, and governments benefit from environmentally friendly products/services and social contribution activities, creating a win-win situation.

Companies that excel in CSR also gain a competitive edge internationally. In 2010, the International Organization for Standardization (ISO) introduced the standard guideline for CSR, 'ISO 26000'. Many experts predict that ISO 26000 will become an international standard and act as a non-tariff trade barrier in international commerce. The UN has enacted the UN Global Compact (UNGC) to encourage companies to enhance their accountability and transparency in human rights, labor, environment, and anti-corruption. It has also introduced Social Responsible Investment (SRI) principles, recommending that governments and financial institutions invest in companies committed to CSR when managing pension funds. Moreover, the OECD is focused on establishing norms related to corporate activities through the OECD Guidelines for Multinational Enterprises, the Convention on Combating Bribery of Foreign Public Officials in International Transactions, and the Principles on Corporate Governance *(Reference: CSR Necessity/Small and Medium Venture 24* (www.smes.go.kr)*).*

There is no need to delve into the detailed international status of Corporate Social Responsibility (CSR) to understand that companies must fulfill their social responsibilities. Companies impact numerous stakeholders—including workers, consumers, local communities, civic groups, and governments—and neglecting their social responsibilities can lead to unforeseen and unfortunate events.

In the 1990s, global sports brand Nike faced severe criticism for exploiting child labor in third-world countries. The American current affairs photo magazine *Life* reported on a 12-year-old boy in Sialkot, Pakistan, who was making soccer balls for 6 cents an hour. Many children, like him, were exploited for low wages and exposed to hazardous substances. The exposure of these facts led to a boycott movement across the United States, with consumers refusing to purchase Nike products made by exploiting children. Moreover, the detection of toluene—a toxic substance—at levels up to 177 times higher than the legal standard in a Nike subcontractor factory in Vietnam also attracted criticism.

As news of Nike's inhumane and immoral practices spread, consumer backlash was fierce, and the company's sales and stock price suffered significantly. The intense public outcry eventually compelled Nike to take corrective actions. The company promised to ban child labor and improve poor working conditions. It introduced the Manufacturing Leadership Partner (MLP) system and maintained subcontracting relationships only with companies that met strict evaluation criteria. Additionally, Nike established the Office of Corporate Responsibility to create and manage guidelines related to worker safety and health, management attitudes, human resource development, and the environment.

Today, Nike is regarded as one of the most active participants in the UN Global Compact and is recognized for its various social contribution activities benefiting local communities and the global society *(Reference: Nike, Criticizing Third World Child Labor Exploiters, Going Beyond ESG, Mediapia, December 28, 2022).*

On the other hand, there are companies like Patagonia that have consistently adhered to their social responsibilities and received praise from consumers. Patagonia, an American eco-friendly outdoor brand, produces equipment and clothing for mountaineering, mountain biking, surfing, skiing, and fly fishing. The brand is renowned for its mission statement, "We are in business to restore our home, the Earth." In alignment with this mission, Patagonia discloses product information and the entire production process—including pollution and waste generated, and energy used—through its "Footprint Chronicle" website.

Furthermore, in 2011, Patagonia promoted the philosophy of avoiding excessive consumption to protect the environment with its counterintuitive "Don't buy this jacket" advertisement. This campaign was refreshingly shocking as it discouraged purchasing to emphasize environmental protection, an unusual stance for a company whose profitability depends on selling products.

Patagonia's products are known for their high quality and higher price point, which result from the use of organic and eco-friendly materials. For their down jackets, they use feathers from slaughtered geese. Additionally, Patagonia Provisions, a non-profit food brand launched by Patagonia, adheres to the principles of organic farming, eco-friendliness, and animal welfare in its products.

Founder and Chairman Yvon Chouinard, who has lived frugally his entire life, made headlines in 2022 when he announced the donation of all of the company's shares, valued at over 4 trillion won, to environmental groups and non-profit organizations. Despite suggestions from close associates to sell Patagonia or take it public, Chouinard declined, believing that prioritizing profits would compromise the company's commitment to environmental protection and employee welfare. Patagonia's steadfast approach to Corporate Social Responsibility (CSR) serves as a global model and has garnered widespread acclaim.

The cases of Nike and Patagonia highlight the crucial role of corporate social responsibility (CSR). A company focused on positive influence can drive significant change and development. Conversely, a profit-centric approach can lead to detrimental outcomes for many people, underlining why the importance of CSR continues to grow daily. Business leaders must reflect seriously on the role their companies play in society.

When SCL employees discussed memorable moments from their social contribution activities, they shared insightful observations. They were particularly moved by how staff at the local children's center tenderly cared for the children, mindful of protecting the children's privacy and emotional well-being during events. This careful consideration made the SCL employees deeply respect The approach of the center, recognizing the staff's focus on truly needed support rather than superficial aid.

This thoughtful approach is what companies should emulate in their social contribution efforts. Rather than using social contributions as a platform for self-promotion, companies should prioritize the genuine needs of those they aim to help, sharing compassion before material support. SCL is committed to continuing its robust program of social contributions. Fulfilling social responsibility means looking beyond profit to collaborate with other community members, creating a world where everyone can thrive. If more companies adopt this mindset, our society will shift towards a more positive direction.

About the Translator: Guihwa H. Blanz

Guihwa H. Blanz worked as a journalist for the New York Korean language daily newspapers prior to working as a translator and is currently active at the translation agency. Ms. Blanz has translated over 200 Korean language books including the Korean record-breaking bestseller, *Youth, It's Painful*.